This Text Book is useful for Savitribai Phule Pune University and other Universities of Maharashtra as well as Competitive Exams.

Political Science

Western Political Thought

(POL - 501 MJ)

M.A. - I (Sem. - I)

As per New Education Policy (2020)

Dr. Meenal Kshirsagar
(M.A., M.Phil., Ph.D.)
Dr. D. Y. Patil Arts, Commerce and Science College, Pune.

2023

Price - 105/

SUCCESS PUBLICATIONS

Published by
Dr. Rajesh M. Patne
Success Publications
Radha Krishna Apartment, 535, Shaniwar Peth,
Appa Balwant Chowk, Opp. Prabhat Talkies, Pune - 411 030.
Ph. 24434662, Mobile : 9325315464.

Edition
2023

Edited By
Mr. Valmik Gaikwad

Typesetting, Layout
Mr. Valmik Gaikwad

Cover Designing
Miss. Varsha Lokhande

ISBN NO. – 978-81-19180-68-4

Preface

It is a matter of great pleasure for us to present this book to our esteemed readers. This book has been designed as standard text on 'Western Political Thought' for M. A. (Political Science) (Sem. - I).

This book comprehensively covers the entire syllabus of M. A. (Political Science) Course of Savitribai Phule Pune University effective from 2023 onwards. It has been written to meet the requirements of students of M. A. (Political Science). Some of the special features of the book are as follows:

1. *Full coverage of the revised syllabus of M. A. (Political Science).*
2. *Chapter outline at the beginning of each chapter to give a bird's eye view of the topics covered in the chapter.*
3. *Point wise explanation of each topic in the chapter.*
4. *Topics are logically arranged in numbered paragraphs exactly according to the modified syllabus.*
5. *Proposed questions at the end of each chapter.*
6. *Extensive use of diagrams, tables and various forms to give visual view of key concepts and techniques.*
7. *Conversational, lucid and simple language.*

Every effort has been made to provide the readers with most up-to-date and authentic material on the subject.

We are very grateful to our publisher Mrs. and Mr. Rajesh Patne who have rendered all possible assistance in bringing out this book. We wish to acknowledge our deep gratitude to staff who have assisted and helped us in preparing this book. We will consider our efforts amply rewarded in case the book proves useful to the students and teachers of the subject.

Suggestions of readers are welcome and shall be acknowledged with gratitude.

With best wishes.

By Authors

Syllabus

M. A. – I (Sem. - I) Political Science
Western Political Thought (POL-501 MJ)

Unit	Topic
1	**Plato**
	a. Life and Works b. Concept of Ideal State c. Theory of Justice d. Views on System of Education
2	**Thomas Hobbes**
	a. Life and Works b. Human Nature and State of Nature c. Views on Natural Rights d. Theory of Social Contract
3	**John Stuart Mill**
	a. Life and Works b. Liberty c. Representative Government d. Views on Utilitarianism
4	**Karl Marx**
	a. Life and Works b. State and Class c. Historical Materialism d. Vies on Revolution

INDEX

M. A. – I (Sem. - I) Political Science
Western Political Thought (POL-501 MJ)

Unit 1

Plato

Introduction:

The Athenian philosopher Plato (c.428-347 B.C.) is one of the most important figures of the Ancient Greek world and the entire history of Western thought. In his written dialogues he conveyed and expanded on the ideas and techniques of his teacher Socrates. The Academy he founded was by some accounts the world's first university and in it he trained his greatest student, the equally influential philosopher Aristotle. Plato's recurring fascination was the distinction between ideal forms and everyday experience, and how it played out both for individuals and for societies. In the "Republic," his most famous work, he envisioned a civilisation governed not by lowly appetites but by the pure wisdom of a philosopher-king.

1.1 Life and Works of Plato:

The Athenian philosopher Plato (c.428-347 B.C.) is one of the most important figures of the Ancient Greek world and the entire history of Western thought. In his written dialogues he conveyed and expanded on the ideas and techniques of his teacher Socrates. The Academy he founded was by some accounts the world's first university and in it he trained his greatest student, the equally influential philosopher Aristotle. Plato's recurring fascination was the distinction between ideal forms and everyday experience, and how it played out both for individuals and for societies. In the "Republic," his most famous work, he envisioned a civilisation governed not by lowly appetites but by the pure wisdom of a philosopher-king.

1.1.1 Life of Plato:

Plato was an ancient Greek philosopher, the second of the trio of ancient Greeks including Socrates and Aristotle said to have laid the philosophical foundations of Western culture. Little can be known about Plato's early life and education due to the very limited accounts. Plato came from one of the wealthiest and most politically active families in Athens. Ancient sources describe him as a bright though modest boy who excelled in his studies. His father contributed everything necessary to give to his son a good education, and Plato therefore must have been instructed in grammar, music, gymnastics and philosophy by some of the most distinguished teachers of his era.

1) Birthdate and Birthplace:

The specific birthdate of Plato is not known. Based on ancient sources, most modern scholars estimate that Plato was born between 428 and 427 BC. The grammarian Apollodorus of Athens argues in his *Chronicles* that Plato was born in the first year of the eighty-eighth Olympiad (427 BC), on the seventh day of the month Thargelion; according to this tradition the god Apollo was born this day. According to another biographer of him, Neanthes, Plato was eighty-four years of age at his death. If we accept Neanthes' version, Plato was younger than Isocrates by six years, and therefore he was born in the second year of the 87th Olympiad, the year Pericles died (429 BC).

The *Chronicle* of Eusebius names the fourth year of the 89th Olympiad as Plato's, when Stratocles was archon, while the *Alexandrian Chronicle* mentions the eighty-ninth Olympiad, in the archonship of Isarchus. According to Suda, Plato was born in Aegina in the 88th Olympiad amid the preliminaries of the Peloponnesian war, and he lived 82 years. Sir Thomas Browne also believes that Plato was born in the 88th Olympiad. Renaissance Platonists celebrated Plato's birth on November 7. Ulrich von Wilamowitz-Moellendorff estimates that Plato was born when Diotimos was archon eponymous, namely between July 29 428 BC and July 24 427 BC. Greek philologist Ioannis Kalitsounakis believes that the philosopher was born on May 26 or 27, 427 BC, while Jonathan Barnes regards 428 BC as year of Plato's birth. For her part, Debra Nails asserts that the philosopher was born in 424/423 BC.

Plato's birthplace is also disputed. Diogenes Laërtius states that Plato "was born, according to some writers, in Aegina in the house of Phidiades the son of Thales". Diogenes mentions as one of his sources the *Universal History* of Favorinus. According to Favorinus, Ariston and his family were sent by Athens to settle as cleruchs (colonists retaining their Athenian citizenship), on the island of Aegina, from which they were expelled by the Spartans after Plato's birth there. Nails points out, however, that there is no record of any Spartan expulsion of Athenians from Aegina between 431 and 411 BC. On the other hand, at the Peace of Nicias,

Aegina was silently left under Athens control, and it was not until the summer of 411 that the Spartans overran the island. Therefore, Nails concludes that "perhaps Ariston was a cleruch, perhaps he went to Aegina in 431, and perhaps Plato was born on Aegina, but none of this enables a precise dating of Ariston's death (or Plato's birth)". Aegina is regarded as Plato's place of birth by Suda as well.

2) Family:

Plato's father was Ariston, of the deme of Colytus. According to a tradition, reported by Diogenes Laërtius but disputed by Wilamowitz-Moellendorff, Ariston traced his descent from the king of Athens, Codrus, and the king of Messenia, Melanthus. That claim is not however exploited in the philosopher's dialogues. Plato's mother was Perictione, whose family boasted of a relationship with the famous Athenian lawmaker and lyric poet Solon. Perictione was sister of Charmides and cousin of Critias, both prominent figures of the Thirty Tyrants, the brief oligarchic regime, which followed on the collapse of Athens at the end of the Peloponnesian war (404–403 BC).

Besides Plato himself, Ariston and Perictione had three other children; these were two sons, Adeimantus and Glaucon, and a daughter, Potone, the mother of Speusippus (the nephew and successor of Plato as head of his philosophical Academy). According to the *Republic*, Adeimantus and Glaucon were older than Plato; the two brothers distinguished themselves in the Battle of Megara, when Plato could not have been more than 5 years old. Nevertheless, in his *Memorabilia*, Xenophon presents Glaucon as younger than Plato.

Ariston appears to have died in Plato's childhood, although the precise dating of his death is difficult. When Ariston died, Athenian law forbade the legal independence of women, and, therefore Perictione was given to marriage to Pyrilampes, her mother's brother's (Plato himself calls him the uncle of Charmides), who had served many times as an ambassador to the Persian court and was a friend of Pericles, the leader of the democratic faction in Athens. Pyrilampes had a son from a previous marriage, Demos, who was famous for his beauty. Perictione gave birth to Pyrilampes' second son, Antiphon, the half-brother of Plato, who appears in *Parmenides*, where he is said to have given up philosophy, in order to devote most of his time to horses. Thus Plato was reared in a household of at least six children, where he was number five: a stepbrother, a sister, two brothers and a half-brother.

In contrast to his reticence about himself, Plato used to introduce his distinguished relatives into his dialogues, or to mention them with some precision: Charmides has one named after him; Critias speaks in both *Charmides* and *Protagoras*; Adeimantus and Glaucon take prominent parts in the *Republic*. From these and other references one can reconstruct his family tree, and this suggests a considerable amount of family pride. According to John Burnet, "the opening scene of the *Charmides* is a glorification of the whole [family] connection ... Plato's dialogues are not only a memorial to Socrates, but also the happier days of his own family".

3) **Name:**

According to Diogenes, the philosopher was named after his grandfather Aristocles, but his wrestling coach, Ariston of Argos, dubbed him "Platon", meaning "broad" on account of his robust figure. Diogenes mentions three sources for the name of Plato (Alexander Polyhistor, Neanthes of Cyzicus and unnamed sources), according to which the philosopher derived his name from the breadth of his eloquence, or else because he was very wide across the forehead. All these sources of Diogenes date from the Alexandrian period of biography which got much of its information from its Peripatetic forerunners. Recent scholars have disputed Diogenes, and argued that *Plato* was the original name of the philosopher, and that the legend about his name being *Aristocles* originated in the Hellenistic age. W. K. C. Guthrie points out that *Plato* was a common name in ancient Greece, of which 31 instances are known at Athens alone.

4) **Legends:**

According to certain fabulous reports of ancient writers, Plato's mother became pregnant from a divine vision: Ariston tried to force his attentions on Perictione, but failed of his purpose; then the ancient Greek god Apollo appeared to him in a vision, and, as a result of it, Ariston left Perictione unmolested. When she had given birth to Plato, only then did her husband lie with her. Another legend related that, while he was sleeping as an infant on Mount Hymettus in a bower of myrtles (his parents were sacrificing to the Muses and Nymphs), bees had settled on the lips of Plato; an augury of the sweetness of style in which he would discourse philosophy.

5) **Education:**

Apuleius informs us that Speusippus praised Plato's quickness of mind and modesty as a boy, and the "first fruits of his youth infused with hard work and love of study". Later Plato himself would characterize as gifts of nature the facility in learning, the memory, the sagacity, the quickness of apprehension and their accompaniments, the youthful spirit and the magnificence in soul. According to Diogenes, Plato's education, like any other Athenian boy's, was physical as well as mental; he was instructed in grammar (that is, reading and writing), music, painting, and gymnastics by the most distinguished teachers of his time. He excelled so much in physical exercises that Dicaearchus went so far as to say, in the first volume of his *Lives*, that Plato wrestled at the Isthmian games and did extremely well and was well known. Apuleius argues that the philosopher went also into a public contest at the Pythian Games. Plato had also attended courses of philosophy; before meeting Socrates, he first became acquainted with Cratylus (a disciple of Heraclitus, a prominent pre-Socratic Greek philosopher) and the Heraclitean doctrines.

According to the ancient writers, there was a tradition that Plato's favorite employment in his youthful years was poetry. He wrote poems, dithyrambs at first, and afterwards lyric poems and tragedies (a tetralogy), but abandoned his early passion and burnt his poems when he met Socrates and turned to philosophy. There was also a story that on the day Plato was entrusted to him, Socrates said that a swan had been delivered to him. There are also some epigrams attributed to Plato, but these are now thought by some scholars to be spurious. Modern scholars now believe that Plato was probably a young boy when he became acquainted with Socrates. This assessment is based on the fact that Critias and Charmides, two close relatives of Plato, were both friends of Socrates.

6) **Public Affairs**:

According to the Seventh Letter, whose authenticity has been disputed, as Plato came of age, he imagined for himself a life in public affairs. He was actually invited by the regime of the Thirty Tyrants (Critias and Charmides were among their leaders) to join the administration, but he held back; he hoped that under the new leadership the city would return to justice, but he was soon repelled by the violent acts of the regime. He was particularly disappointed, when the Thirty attempted to implicate Socrates in their seizure of the democratic general Leon of Salamis for summary execution.

In 403 BC, the democracy was restored after the regrouping of the democrats in exile, who entered the city through the Piraeus and met the forces of the Thirty at the Battle of Munychia, where both Critias and Charmides were killed. In 401 BC the restored democrats raided Eleusis and killed the remaining oligarchic supporters, suspecting them of hiring mercenaries. After the overthrow of the Thirty, Plato's desire to become politically active was rekindled, but Socrates' condemnation to death put an end to his plans. In 399 BC, Plato and other Socratic men took temporary refuge at Megara with Euclid, founder of the Megarian school of philosophy.

1.1.2 Works of Plato:

Prior to understanding Plato's writings, it is in fact important to comprehend the method adopted by him in his writings. It is important to acquire some knowledge of his philosophy as a whole. Most often, a philosopher provides an explanation and thereby theorizes.

The reader is expected to understand and analyze and absorb the essence of it. Plato, unlike the others, pursued a dialogue method, which was mostly politico-philosophical in nature. One significant feature of Plato's dialogues was the use of analogies. His analogies from nature are drawn from the brutal world. Plato believed that politics is an art and in its pursuit, there should be knowledge.

The statesmen should know what he is pursuing. Plato was of the opinion that the statesmen should ideally be free from the restraint of law and advocate a theory of absolute monarchy. Plato argued that just as the artist must work for the improvements of his artistic skills, statesmen should also work for the welfare of his subjects.

Further, Plato followed a deductive method, which made him the first Utopian philosopher. He never bothered about the origin of the state or the bases of an ideal state in realistic terms. He never paid any attention to the feasibility of such an ideal state. Thus, realism went away from the philosophy of Plato.

1) Literature of Plato:

The Greek political thought was greatly enriched by the fertile philosophical literature of Plato. He wrote a number of works, but the most important are Apology, Crito, Phaedo, Symposium, The Republic, Statesmen and The Laws.

a) Apology was written after the death of Socrates in 399 BC. It is related to the circumstances that eventually led to the death of his teacher.

b) Crito, another work, was a kind of dialogue related to the trial and death of Socrates. Crito, in fact, was a friend of Socrates.

c) Phaedo, the third work of Plato is a description of Socrates in his last days in a cell all alone. It was a beautiful blend of high drama and high philosophy relating to the immortality of the human soul.

d) Symposium, the fifth major work, was also a platonic philosophy of love.

e) The Republic was the masterpiece of Plato that made him immortal in the field of philosophy. According to Gettel, Plato attempted to establish the philosophic conceptions of justice, and in doing so, he set forth his conception of ideal state in which justice prevails. The point of view is primarily ethical and idealistic. It was described as a matchless introduction to the basic issues that confront human beings as citizens.

The Republic was universally acclaimed as one of the greatest works of all times. It was written when Plato was around 40 years. The Republic comprised of nearly 10 books that dealt with certain moral and philosophical principles. It encompasses a variety of problems related to morality, metaphysics, sociology, education and so on. The book begins with a proposition; what a good man is? And how can one become so? Eventually, it leads to the question, what is a good state? Finally, Statesmen and

f) The Laws were the later works of Plato, which reflect the problems of the city-states. The two works belong to the last days of Plato at a time when his Academy failed to meet his expectations. This made him realize that his schemes were Utopian and visionary in nature. Thus, the last two works of Plato clearly reflect his disillusionment.

2) **He is Credited with Establishing the First University in Europe:**
In *399 BCE,* after *Socrates was sentenced to death*, Plato left *Athens*. It is believed that he traveled extensively during this period, and returned 12 years later in 387 BCE. There is no historical record of the exact time Plato's school was officially founded, but modern scholars generally agree that the time was *mid-380s BCE;* after his return. *The Akademia* or *the Academy*was a school outside the city walls of ancient Athens. It was a place where students would study a wide variety of subjects from various instructors. The Academy is accredited by most scholars to be *the first known university in Europe*. It attracted many brilliant men including *Theaetetus* (mathematician), *Eudoxus of Cnidus* (mathematician) and *Aristotle* (philosopher). Plato believed such institutions would lead to social progress and a more stable government and he *oversaw the Academy until he died in 347 BCE*. The Academy was *destroyed* in *86 BC E*after the siege of Athens by the Roman dictator *Sulla*. Almost 500 years later in *410 AD* a revived *Neoplatonic Academy* was established as a center for Neoplatonism and mysticism until 529 when it was closed down by the Christian Emperor *Justinian I*, who claimed it was a*pagan establishment*.

3) **He gave us an Insight into the Philosophical Teachings of Socrates:**
Socrates is credited as *being among the founders of Western Philosophical thought* and is often designated as the *first moral philosopher* by historians. Although Socrates was an influential thinker during his times, he *did not write down any of his teachings*. Socrates is thus known through the writings of his contemporaries like *Antisthenes* and *Aristippus* or his student's like*Xenophon* and Plato, among others. Plato for the most part wrote in dialogues in which characters discuss a subject analyzing and dissecting it from various viewpoints. In what are known as *"dialogues"*, the early writings of Plato seem to be *directly inherited from Socrates*. Plato's teacher Socrates is mostly the central character in these writings with subjects usually centered on Socrates' lessons. The most famous of the Socratic Dialogues is the *Apology*in which the character of Socrates defends his beliefs against the charges of the Athenian court. Although other sources portray a different Socrates, Plato's "dialogues" are a *vital source for understanding Socrates.*

4) **He Wrote Numerous Philosophical Discussions Which Continue to be debated:**
Plato's Dialogues
Scholars typically organize Plato's works into three different eras:-
Early period - writings attributed to him in this period include *Apology of Socrates, Euthyphro, Hippias Major and Minor,* and *Ion.* The fictional character of Socrates in the dialogues is *an integral part* of this period.
Middle Period - most famous works attributed to Plato were written during this time, including the *Republic,* the *Symposium* and *Phaedo.* Plato continues to use his

dialogues to explore philosophical concepts such as government, love and the soul. During this era, the character of Socrates *still remains a fictional vehicle to argue philosophical concepts* but he starts to *recede into the background.*

Late Period - most famous creative works of this period are *Parmenides* and *Theaetetus.* In this period, Plato questions the paradoxes of religion and knowledge.

A majority of Plato's work is in the form of dialogues, which many times *do not lead to any conclusion.* A student of Plato's philosophy is encouraged to approach a topic in many different ways and repeatedly question the result. These dramatic features of Plato's works have earned attention even from literary scholars relatively uninterested in philosophy and are the reason that they continue to be hotly debated after many years.

5) **He came up with the Influential Theory of Forms:**

The *concept of forms* is *central to the philosophy of Plato.* However, some attribute the philosophy to Socrates. The concept talks of *an ideal world of Forms* which are *mimicked* in the *false world of phenomena.* The phenomena are the *physical world that we experience*; it is a *flawed echo of the perfect, ideal model that exists outside of space and time.* Taking a simple example of a physical object like a chair or a concept like justice, it can be loosely said that we experience an imperfect chair and imperfect justice in the phenomena or the material world we exist in. However there is an ideal and perfect chair and justice in the ideal world of Forms. Forms are used throughout the work of Plato to explain concepts of knowledge, justice and many others. In his work Republic, Plato is said to have demonstrated this concept of the Forms in an illustration called *The Allegory of the Cave.*

6) **He came up with Epistemology or Theory of Knowledge:**

Plato believed that *true knowledge may only be derived from world of ideal and timeless forms.* As an example in his Socratic dialogue Meno, a boy is able to find mathematical truths without observation of the world, arriving at the truth by being asked questions and considering the answers. Plato claims it as an example of recollection with the ultimate truths in a past life or knowledge by contemplation rather than observation. He argues that knowledge is *inherently present in a person's soul* and is *shrouded by their perception of reality.*

7) **His Work Republic is regarded as a Cornerstone of Western Philosophy:**

Republic is perhaps the *most known and influential work of Plato* on philosophy and politics. Essentially a Socratic dialogue on Justice, Republic explores *a philosophical conversation between 6 men on an ideal state (Republic) that would serve as a template for all existing and emerging societies.* In Republic, the four virtues of courage, wisdom, temperance and justice are recommended for a good community and among them Plato reasons that justice is the most important.

8) He Propagated Division of Labor:

Plato identified the *human need* as the *fundamental cause of association*. He thought that people essentially serve their own self-interests; they organize and support each other as it seems to be in one's self-interest. Plato advocated *division of labor* to organize productive efforts. He thought that every individual had different natural ability and therefore was suited to one occupation as another may be suited to something else. He believed that for many things to be done at the same time, it required availability of some people fixed for some tasks.

He reasoned that the society be divided into three classes:

a) The *"appetite" of the soul* or the workers that *produce for consumption* like the laborers, merchants, farmers etc.

b) The *"spirit" of the soul* or the *strong and brave guardians* that protect.

c) The *"reason" of the soul* or rulers or philosopher kings who are *intelligent, rational, self-controlled and in love with wisdom and justice.*

Plato said that only through specialization in one of these duties can disunity between people be erased and a just state is established.

9) Plato laid Emphasis on Education:

Plato recognized that *only through education can an individual realize his true function in society*. In Republic, education is considered *only second to justice for the creation of an ideal state*. Plato advocated state controlled education and is against any form of forced learning. Education is looked upon as the art of orientation and educators are encouraged to device simple methods to align learning in the right direction.

10) He came up with the Influential Concept of Platonic Love:

In his work *Symposium*, Plato offers insight into the *philosophy of love and beauty*. In this philosophical fiction 7 characters give speeches in the praise of *Eros*, the *god of love and desire*. Plato explores various viewpoints through these characters. The character Socrates discusses how men should start with the love of a particular beautiful person, in the next step love is a particular instance of beauty in general, and then love shifts from physical to moral beauty. One should have the love of wisdom as the next step, and finally be able to love and appreciate the divine beauty. It is said that herein lays the first seeds of what we know as *Platonic Love* today, a type of an *emotional and spiritual companionship without sexual desire*.

11) He was a Leading Mentor of Mathematics of his Time:

Although Plato was not a mathematician himself, he was among the *important patrons of the subject* in ancient Greece. Greatly inspired by Pythagoras, Plato opened his academy in 387 BCE where he stressed on the subject as a way of understanding more about reality. It is said that his Academy trained *some of the most prominent mathematicians of ancient Europe* like *Eudoxus, Theaetetus* and *Archytas*.

1.2 Concept of Ideal State:

In his most celebrated book the Republic, Plato gives the theory of an ideal state. As far as a state is concerned, Plato gives ideas about how to build an Ideal commonwealth, who should be the rulers of the Ideal state and how to achieve justice in the Ideal state. Plato finds the state as the more suitable place to discuss about the morality than an individual, because everything is easier to see in the large than in the small. A state says Plato, is a man 'writ' large against the sky. The elements that make up a city correspond to the elements that constitute the individual human soul. Plato's notion of the "philosopher king" and the rigid social order necessary to sustain such institution, is an ill advice to any political entity that aspires to be rules-based, diverse, pluralist and open to socio cultural change. Nonetheless, Plato's ideas are not altogether incompatible with contemporary modes of political organisation. A constituted, law-governed society that makes use of scientific input in the formulation of its policies can be considered as partly subscribing to an adaptation of Plato's program, in so far as it sets to pursue a range of substantive moral objectives for the totality of its citizen.

Plato constructs his Ideal State in three successive 'waves'. In the first wave, he shows that men and women should have the same education and should partake in the same public functions. In the second wave, he advocates the abolition of the family on the basis of communism of wives and property among the two upper classes. The third wave is concerned with the idea that the salvation of society depends on government by Philosopher kings. Plato's Ideal State is hierarchical in its composition and functioning.

A) Features of Ideal State:

Following are the features of Plato's ideal state:

1) Rule of Philosophy:

According to Plato, "If political power and scientific knowledge (philosophy) are not united in one person, then there is no end of evil for the States and also for mankind in general". According to him, his Ideal State will be guided by eternal ideas and the life is to be governed by the absolute ideas. This life of becoming is to be made life of being. Only philosophers can understand these ideas. Hence, the ruler will be able to rule the State according to these ideas. Reason will dominate as the chief quality of the Philosopher-guardians. So at the head of Plato's Ideal State there is a Philosopher-ruler who would be the embodiment of reason and therefore, virtue in action, whose wise and beneficent rule is untrammelled by the restraints of law. This implies that the philosopher-ruler knows the art of statesmanship and state-craft. A Philosopher King is a true statesman and his monarchy is the best form of Government. He has the decisive power in Government and it is his knowledge alone which entitles him to the position. His knowledge is at once his right and duty to rule. The Philosopher-rulers are according to Plato, the men of gold, whom nature has given birth to rule.

2) State Regulated Education:

Plato suggests a well regulated scheme of education under state control in order to ensure a constant supply of philosophers-guardians. State was, to him, to be mainly an educational institution. All the rulers must pass through this established and State controlled system of training and education. They are trained to acquire higher knowledge. The curriculum is to be consisted of subjects such as Mathematics, Astronomy, Logic and Dialectics. In the elementary education, he includes training in gymnastics and music for the perfection of body and mind. This system is to train individuals from their boyhood upto the age of 35 and thus they become real and true philosophers of the design which Plato desires. Moreover, it would be possible to shift the capable from the incapable. Plato takes care to divide the guardian class into perfect guardians "who preserve as against foreign enemies and maintain peace among our citizens at home" and auxiliaries or administrators who are mere supporters of the perfect guardians.

3) Communism of Wives and Property:

Plato is of the opinion that the philosopher, freed from the cares of his family and private property will devote more attention to the affairs of the state and to the cultivation and acquisition of sound knowledge. The communism of wives and property among the upper classes i.e., guardian classes was meant to keep them out of the economic and worldly temptations and ambitions so that they could concentrate on their duty to the State.

4) Vocational Specialisation:

Plato divides the whole community into three classes or professions. Firstly, there is the class of philosopher guardians i.e., perfect rulers representing Reason. They are fit for the highest duties of statesmanship. Secondly, there were ordinary guardians i.e., auxiliaries and administrators representing the element of spirit. Lastly, there are non- guardians i.e., common people. They are otherwise called producing class, cut up into a number of sections such as artisans and farmers, each with its own special work. The specialisation of functions is based on two factors natural aptitude and training. The first is innate and the second is matter of experience and education.

5) Justice:

Justice is a cornerstone of Plato's Ideal State. To him, a State was Ideal if justice reigns supreme in it. The philosopher ruler knows what justice is. He should foster justice in an appropriate manner. According to him, unity and harmony will prevail in the State because of justice and it is inseparable from his Ideal State. It grows with the specialisation of functions. The justice of the State is the citizen's sense of duty.

6) **Equality of Men and Women:**

Plato gives same status to men and women in his Ideal State. To him, the day of emancipation of women will be the day of unity of the State, liberty to the individual and justice to both. He gives his whole hearted support for this. He plans to give the same education to both sexes.

7) **Censorship of Art and Literature:**

The Ideal State of Plato is absolute and totalitarian. Plato is no apostle of freedom of thought and association. Even the art and literature which goes against the interest of the State must be destroyed. He advocates a strict censorship of art and literature. To him, the State is Ideal and is ruled by supreme wisdom.

B) Criticism on Ideal State:

Here are some key criticisms of Plato's ideal state:

1) **Authoritarianism and Lack of Individual Freedom:**

One of the most common criticisms of Plato's ideal state is its potential for authoritarianism. The strict class hierarchy, communal property, and centralized decision-making by philosopher-kings raise concerns about individual autonomy and freedom. Critics argue that the ideal state's structure limits personal choices and suppresses individual creativity and diversity.

2) **Lack of Practicality:**

Many critics point out that Plato's ideal state is more of a philosophical construct than a practical blueprint for real-world governance. The stringent requirements for philosopher-kings and the implementation of communalism are often deemed unrealistic. The complexities of governing a large and diverse population are not adequately addressed in Plato's vision.

3) **Disconnection from Reality:**

Plato's focus on the realm of Forms and abstract concepts can lead to a disconnection from the real world. Critics argue that his emphasis on the pursuit of truth and philosophical knowledge neglects the practicalities of addressing immediate social and economic needs.

4) **Neglect of Material and Economic Concerns:**

Plato's ideal state places a significant emphasis on the realm of ideas, virtue, and justice, often at the expense of material and economic considerations. Critics argue that a state cannot thrive without addressing practical economic matters, such as production, distribution, and wealth creation.

5) **Suppression of Diversity and Individuality:**

The emphasis on specialization and the rigid class structure in Plato's ideal state can lead to the suppression of individuality and diversity. Critics argue that a society where individuals are assigned roles based on their innate abilities restricts personal development and the pursuit of diverse talents.

6) **Philosopher-King Problem:**

The idea of philosopher-kings ruling the state raises concerns about who decides who qualifies as a philosopher-king and how they would be selected. Critics question whether those with philosophical knowledge would necessarily make good political leaders, and whether such leaders could resist the temptations of power.

7) **Impractical Education System:**

Plato's education system, while aiming to cultivate wisdom and virtue, may be seen as overly prescriptive and one-size-fits-all. Critics argue that individuals have diverse learning styles and needs, and the rigid education system proposed by Plato might not suit everyone.

8) **Gender and Family Issues:**

Plato's proposal to abolish family structures within the guardian class and treat women equally as warriors and rulers has faced criticism for being unrealistic and for not considering the complexities of human relationships and social dynamics.

9) **Potential for Totalitarianism:**

The concentration of power in the hands of philosopher-kings can lead to a totalitarian regime, where dissent and opposition are suppressed in the name of the common good. Critics argue that the absence of checks and balances can pave the way for tyranny.

10) **Ethical Concerns:**

Plato's ideal state raises ethical concerns related to the coercion of individuals into prescribed roles, the disregard for individual desires and choices, and the potential for harm caused by the state's intervention in personal matters.

1.3 Theory of Justice:

Plato propounds his own theory of justice which is true and final through the person of Socrates. He gives extraordinary importance to justice, as is obvious from the subtitle of his best dialogue, The Republic, because he saw injustice, the only remedy against the political and social ills of his beloved city-state Athens. Justice, according to Plato resides in the ideally constituted community and is identifiable with complete virtue which consists of four virtues, i.e., wisdom (Philosophers), courage (which includes strength of will), obedience and discipline (soldiers), temperance or self-control and justice. To Plato "Justice is the virtue which remains in the state when the other virtues of temperance and courage and wisdom are abstracted and is the ultimate cause and condition of the existence of all of them." The conception of justice is inseparable from that of the Ideal State. The two blend in one and cannot be isolated Justice is the order, i.e., the true condition of the state and the Ideal State is the visible embodiment of justice. The one is the soul, the other the body-fair mind in a fair body.

A good and just life is one lived in society and justice demands an organic unity in the state arising out of a harmonious balancing of functions of the three classes of society the appetitive, the spirited and the rational and justice in Plato's language means "the will to concentrate on one's own sphere of duty and not to meddle with the sphere of others and its habitation, therefore, is the heart of every citizen who does his duty in his appointed place". Thus, justice depends and grows with the specialisation of functions. The justice of the state is the citizens' sense of duty." To Plato, justice is an indispensable quality of moral life in the community. Platonic justice does not embody a conception of individual rights; it conceives of individual duties. Plato's polity is a moral organism and his theory of justice is a theory of the ethical code by which it lives.

A) Justice in the Individual:

Plato presents his theory of justice through a metaphor known as the **Tripartite Soul**. He divides the human soul into three distinct parts, each corresponding to a specific aspect of human nature:

1) Reason (Rational Part):

The rational part of the soul represents our capacity for critical thinking, wisdom, and logical decision-making. It is associated with the pursuit of truth and knowledge.

2) Spirit (Spirited Part):

The spirited part embodies emotions such as courage, ambition, and assertiveness. It drives our desires for honor, recognition, and competitive achievement.

3) Appetite (Appetitive Part):

The appetitive part is connected to our physical desires and pleasures, including hunger, thirst, and sensual gratification.

According to Plato, **justice within the individual** occurs when these three parts are in harmony and each fulfills its appropriate role:

a) Reason should govern and guide the soul, making rational decisions for the individual's well-being.

b) Spirit should support reason, helping the individual pursue noble goals and defend virtuous principles.

c) Appetite should be moderated and controlled by reason, ensuring that physical desires do not dominate one's life.

When each part performs its function without encroaching on the functions of the others, the individual achieves internal harmony and justice.

B) Justice in the Ideal State:

Plato extends his theory of justice to the concept of justice in the ideal state. He argues that the just state mirrors the just individual, with each class of citizens performing its proper function in society. In the ideal state, justice is achieved through a strict division of labor and roles:

1) Rulers (Philosopher-Kings):

The philosopher-kings represent the rational part of the state. They possess wisdom, knowledge of the Forms, and an unwavering commitment to the pursuit of truth. Their role is to govern & make decision based on the common good & justice.

2) **Guardians:**

The guardian class corresponds to the spirited part of the soul. Guardians are trained warriors who protect the state from external threats. They are characterized by courage, discipline, and a sense of duty.

3) **Producers:**

The producer class corresponds to the appetitive part of the soul. They engage in agricultural, industrial, and commercial activities, ensuring the material needs of the state are met.

C) **Criticisms on Theory:**

Here are some key criticisms of Plato's theory of justice:

1) **Overemphasis on Unity and Harmony:**

Critics argue that Plato's theory places an excessive emphasis on achieving unity and harmony within both the individual and the state. This emphasis might lead to the suppression of individuality, dissenting opinions, and diverse perspectives, potentially stifling creativity and innovation.

2) **Incompatibility with Individual Freedom:**

Plato's vision of the ideal state relies on a strict division of labor and a hierarchy of classes. Critics contend that this hierarchical structure might restrict individual freedom and autonomy. The assigned roles and lack of choice might not align with the principles of individual self-determination.

3) **Lack of Consideration for Diversity:**

Plato's theory of justice assumes a standardized model of virtue and wisdom. Critics argue that this approach does not adequately consider the diversity of human experiences, cultural backgrounds, and differing conceptions of the good life. The theory might not be applicable to societies with diverse values and beliefs.

4) **Elitism and Philosopher-Kings:**

Plato's idea of philosopher-kings ruling the state raises concerns about the concentration of power in the hands of intellectual elite. Critics question whether philosophers possess the practical skills and leadership qualities required for effective governance. This notion of philosopher-kings can be seen as elitist and exclusionary.

5) **Unrealistic Assumptions about Human Nature:**

Plato's theory assumes that individuals will always act in accordance with reason and wisdom, prioritizing the pursuit of truth and justice. Critics argue that this assumption is unrealistic, as human behavior is influenced by emotions, desires, and irrational impulses that might not align with the pursuit of the common good.

6) **Neglect of Material Concerns:**

Plato's focus on justice, virtue, and wisdom sometimes neglects the practicalities of economic and material considerations. Critics contend that a just state must address issues such as production, distribution of resources, and wealth creation to ensure the well-being of its citizens.

7) **Disconnection from Real-World Context:**
Critics point out that Plato's theory of justice is an abstract and idealized construct that may not be applicable to the complex and diverse realities of societies. The theory's lack of engagement with historical, cultural, and socio-economic contexts can limit its practical relevance.

8) **Lack of Political Participation:**
Plato's ideal state restricts political participation to a select few, namely the philosopher-kings and the guardian class. Critics argue that this exclusionary approach denies citizens the opportunity to engage in the democratic process and have a say in the decisions that affect their lives.

9) **Potential for Totalitarianism:**
Plato's emphasis on the philosopher-kings' supreme authority might lead to a form of totalitarianism, where a small group wields unchecked power. Critics worry about the lack of checks and balances and the potential for the rulers to abuse their authority.

D) **The Value of Plato's Theory:**
Inspite of above criticism, Plato's theory of justice is of immense value. It is a kind of thesis against individualism. "The conception postulates a view of the individual as not an isolated self but part of an order, intended not to pursue the pleasure of isolated self but to fill an appointed place in that order." Plato's justice is universal in character and is another name for the whole duty of men. According to Dunning, the Platonic conception of justice "on the political side proper brings out in highest relief first, the necessity of an organic unity in social life; second, the importance of systematic education, as contrasted with the haphazard legislation in regulating the common interest; and third, the national basis of aristocracy in government." Plato's theory bestows upon the state a personality and independent existence of its own. There is no doubt that the theory is a revolt against political selfishness and ignorance. Justice in Plato is a part of human virtue and also a bond of state at the same time. It is that bond which joins man together in society. It makes man both good and social. This identification is the first and the fundamental principle of Plato's political philosophy, according to Foster. 'This conception also gave birth to the organic theory of the state. In a way it also resolves the problem of individual liberty and the Leviathan state. It brings the final identification between the individual and the society to which he is born. The conception is of importance also due to the fact that it brings into prominence two important principles of division of labour and specialisation of function for efficiency and harmony in the state. Moreover, the significance of Plato's theory lies in the fact that it is the forerunner of the psychological explanation of the state.

1.4 Views on System of Education:

Plato's republic is not merely an essay on Justice. It is one of the greatest treatises on education to be ever written. The main objective of Plato's philosophy was to bring about reforms in the Greek city states. The object of the Republic was to locate and thereafter establish justice in the ideal state and his scheme of education is the spiritual remedy for the realisation of justice. According to Plato, social education is a means to social justice. It is; therefore, correct to say that education for Plato has been a solution to all the important questions during his period.

A) Goals of Education:

Plato's educational philosophy was guided by his vision of the ideal state and his pursuit of justice. The overarching goal of education, for Plato, was to cultivate individuals who possessed virtue, wisdom, and a deep understanding of truth and justice. He believed that a just society could only be achieved through the cultivation of just individuals. Education, in his view, was a means to transform the soul and guide individuals toward the pursuit of the highest ideals.

B) Nature of the Soul and Education:

Plato's tripartite theory of the soul, as discussed in "The Republic," played a crucial role in shaping his views on education. He divided the soul into three parts: reason, spirit, and appetite. Education, according to Plato, aimed at harmonizing these parts and ensuring that reason governed the soul. The development of reason was central to cultivating wisdom and virtue, leading to the individual's moral and intellectual growth.

C) Methods of Education:

Plato's educational methods were designed to foster critical thinking, self-discovery, and a deep engagement with truth. His approach can be summarized as follows:

1) Dialectical Inquiry:

Plato emphasized the Socratic method of dialectical questioning as a means to stimulate critical thinking and uncover deeper truths. Through dialogue and inquiry, educators would guide students toward a deeper understanding of concepts, helping them transcend mere opinions and engage with universal principles.

2) Stimulating Intellectual Curiosity:

Plato believed that education should ignite students' curiosity and desire for knowledge. Educators were to present questions and problems that would challenge students' assumptions and encourage them to seek answers independently.

3) Mathematics and Philosophy:

Plato considered mathematics and philosophy as foundational subjects in education. Mathematics cultivated logical reasoning and abstract thinking, while philosophy enabled students to engage with fundamental questions about reality, ethics, and the nature of the soul.

D) Curriculum:

Plato's curriculum was designed to develop both intellectual and moral virtues. His ideal curriculum included:

1) Music and Poetry:

Plato valued music and poetry for their capacity to shape emotions and character. However, he was selective about the content, advocating for the censorship of artistic works that could have a negative influence on morals.

2) Physical Education:

Plato emphasized physical education to develop a strong and disciplined body. Physical training aimed at cultivating courage and self-control, virtues essential for the guardian class in his ideal state.

3) Mathematics:

Mathematics was considered foundational for its role in developing logical thinking and analytical skills. Arithmetic, geometry, astronomy, and harmonics were part of the curriculum.

4) Philosophy:

At the heart of Plato's curriculum was philosophy, which aimed at developing rationality, wisdom, and a deep understanding of truth. Philosophy involved contemplation of the Forms and engagement with metaphysical and ethical questions.

E) Role of Educators:

Educators, in Plato's view, were essential guides who facilitated the intellectual and moral development of students. They were not mere instructors but mentors who guided students toward self-discovery and the pursuit of virtue. Educators were expected to be wise, knowledgeable, and possessed of moral integrity, serving as role models for their students.

F) Education and the Ideal State:

Plato's views on education were intrinsically linked to his vision of the ideal state. He believed that the education of philosopher-kings, who possessed knowledge of the Forms and a deep commitment to justice, was crucial for the governance of the state. The education of the guardian class aimed at fostering virtues like courage, discipline, and a sense of duty. The broader population would receive an education tailored to their roles in society, ensuring that each individual contributed to the common good.

G) Features of Plato's System of Education:

Here are the key features of Plato's system of education:

1) Cultivation of Virtue:

At the core of Plato's educational system is the cultivation of moral and intellectual virtues. He believed that education should shape individuals' characters and guide them toward virtuous behavior. The goal was to harmonize the soul's different parts reason, spirit, and appetite by emphasizing the supremacy of reason and the subordination of desires.

2) **Focus on Philosophy:**

Plato considered philosophy to be the cornerstone of education. He believed that engagement with metaphysical, ethical, and epistemological questions was essential for developing individuals who could think critically and engage deeply with truth. Philosophical inquiry, through dialectical dialogue and contemplation of the Forms, was a central method of education.

3) **Dialectical Inquiry:**

Plato's method of dialectical inquiry, influenced by his teacher Socrates, played a central role in his educational approach. Educators engaged students in rigorous questioning, encouraging them to critically examine their assumptions and develop a deeper understanding of concepts. Dialectical inquiry aimed to move beyond mere opinions and reach a higher level of knowledge.

4) **Pursuit of Truth and Wisdom:**

Plato's educational system aimed to guide individuals toward the pursuit of truth and wisdom. He believed that true knowledge was rooted in an understanding of the eternal and unchanging Forms, which represented the highest reality. Education involved the development of intellectual faculties to grasp these transcendent truths.

5) **Development of Critical Thinking:**

Plato's system emphasized the development of critical thinking skills. Through dialectical questioning and philosophical discourse, students were encouraged to analyze ideas, examine arguments, and evaluate various perspectives. This approach aimed to cultivate a habit of critical reflection that extended beyond the classroom.

6) **Selective Curriculum:**

Plato's curriculum was carefully designed to align with his philosophical goals. It included subjects that nurtured intellectual and moral virtues, such as mathematics, music, and philosophy. Mathematics developed logical reasoning, while music and poetry shaped emotions and character. The curriculum aimed to harmonize the intellectual and emotional aspects of the individual.

7) **Moral Education through Art and Literature:**

Plato recognized the power of art and literature in shaping individuals' values and emotions. He advocated for the censorship of artistic works that promoted negative influences, aiming to ensure that the content of art and literature aligned with the virtues he sought to cultivate.

8) **Division of Labor and Role Differentiation:**

Plato's educational system was tailored to the individual's future role in society. He believed in a strict division of labor, and education was aligned with an individual's natural talents and abilities. Different classes philosopher-kings, guardians, and producers received education appropriate to their roles in the ideal state.

H) Criticisms on Plato's System of Education:

Here are some of the key criticisms of Plato's system of education:

1) Elitism and Exclusivity:

One of the most common criticisms of Plato's system is its potential for elitism. The strict division of classes and the emphasis on producing philosopher-kings and guardians could lead to a society dominated by small intellectual elite. Critics argue that this approach excludes individuals from different backgrounds and fails to address the needs and potential contributions of a diverse population.

2) Censorship of Art and Literature:

Plato's advocacy for the censorship of art and literature has been met with resistance. Critics argue that censoring creative expression limits freedom of speech and stifles artistic creativity. Furthermore, determining what is morally acceptable in art can be subjective and prone to abuse by those in power.

3) Neglect of Practical Skills:

Plato's curriculum focuses heavily on philosophy, mathematics, and music, often neglecting practical skills necessary for daily life and economic productivity. Critics contend that an education system should prepare individuals for a range of practical tasks and professions, rather than prioritizing the pursuit of abstract knowledge.

4) Lack of Individual Autonomy:

Plato's system places significant emphasis on role differentiation and predetermined assignments based on one's natural abilities. Critics argue that this approach limits individual autonomy and self-determination, as students may feel compelled to conform to societal expectations rather than pursuing their own interests and passions.

5) Impracticality of Philosopher-Kings:

The concept of philosopher-kings as rulers has faced skepticism. Critics question whether individuals with philosophical knowledge are inherently suited for political leadership. Leadership requires a range of practical skills, negotiation abilities, and an understanding of complex socio-economic dynamics that might not be directly related to philosophical wisdom.

6) Potential for Totalitarianism:

Critics argue that Plato's concentration of power in the hands of philosopher-kings and guardians raises concerns about the potential for a totalitarian regime. A society where a small group makes all decisions might lead to the suppression of dissent and a lack of checks and balances.

7) Unrealistic Assumptions about Human Nature:

Plato's system assumes that all individuals are motivated by the pursuit of truth and the common good. Critics argue that human behavior is influenced by a range of desires, emotions, and interests that might not align with these ideals. The system's success hinges on the assumption of universal moral alignment.

8) **Lack of Empirical Education:**
Plato's emphasis on abstract knowledge and philosophical contemplation might neglect the importance of empirical education and engagement with the natural world. Critics argue that a well-rounded education should include hands-on experiences, practical skills, and a connection to the physical environment.

9) **Lack of Adaptability to Changing Times:**
Plato's educational system is based on his philosophical and social context. Critics argue that his emphasis on a specific curriculum and a hierarchical society might not be adaptable to the evolving needs and challenges of different societies and historical periods.

10) **Reductionist Approach to Virtue:**
Critics contend that Plato's focus on intellectual virtues and the pursuit of truth might neglect other important aspects of virtue, such as compassion, empathy, and social responsibility. A holistic education should address a wider range of virtues and ethical dimensions.

1.5 Philosopher King:

In Plato's portrayal of the Ideal State, the system of government was a natural corollary of the system of education. The government flowed from education, not education from the government. The government must be directed and controlled by knowledge and because the only true knowledge was philosophy, the government must be controlled by philosophers. According to Plato, only by the rule of the Philosopher, kings can stake a government in which the rulers rule in wisdom and in unselfishness for their eyes have seen the truth and they think of their exalted offices not as opportunities for self-aggrandizement, but as a sacred burden to be home for the good of the ruled.

A) Plato's Conception of a Philosopher:

Plato conceives of a philosopher as "the spectator of all time and all existence". "He has the noblest gills of nature and makes the highest use of them." He is a lover of truth and has always a passion for reality. He hates falsehood and possesses self-control. He is free from all sorts of meanness or spitefulness or little-mindedness. He is just and gentle and shows due proportion in all things. He does not fear death or think much of human life. He has a vision of the unity of knowledge. The Platonic Philosopher must know the "Idea" or essence of justice and of Beauty and Temperance in order that he may fashion with their likeness the characters of those whom he rules, ultimately he must know the "Idea" of which all other Ideas are, but phase and from which the above idea comes as the "Idea of the Good". He must know the purpose of all being and all doing and the end of all human existence and human action.

The Platonic philosopher, however, is not the devoted seeker for wisdom, but its proud possessor he is a learned man and a sage. By the rule of philosophy, Plato means the rule of learnedness or the rule of the intellect. It is in this rule of intellect that the Socratic doctrine of 'knowledge is virtue' is fully realised in its institutional form. According to Popper, "Plato gives the term philosopher a new meaning of a lover and a seer of the divine world of forms or Ideas". It is this philosopher who becomes the virtuous founder of a virtuous city.

B) The Philosopher King:

By creating the philosopher king, Plato made an attempt to create a friend, a philosopher and a guide at the same time that could by leading a life of ascetic simplicity and virtue, inspire confidence among his subjects. Plato's philosopher king is similar to the ancient Indian Maharishi who is the embodiment of all knowledge, all virtue, all beauty and all divinity. Appetite, to Plato, was a social bond, bringing men together for the satisfaction of their wants; spirit gave safety and integrity, but these two were not enough without a regulative force. Uncontrolled appetite would lead to unbridled political and economic individualism and unbridled spirit would produce unmitigated brutes. Reason was necessary regulative force and the philosopher rulers embodied reason.

C) Qualities of the Philosopher-King:

Plato believed that the philosopher-king should possess a unique set of qualities that set them apart as the ideal rulers for the state:

1) Philosophical Wisdom:

The philosopher-king is characterized by their love of wisdom (philosophia) and their pursuit of truth and knowledge. They have transcended the illusions of the material world and have knowledge of the eternal and unchanging Forms.

2) Virtue and Temperance:

The philosopher-king embodies moral virtue and self-discipline. They are not swayed by personal desires and are able to make just decisions for the common good.

3) Detachment from Material Wealth:

The philosopher-king is not motivated by personal gain or material wealth. Their focus is on the welfare of the state and the pursuit of justice.

4) Intellectual Capacity:

The philosopher-king possesses a high level of intellectual capacity and the ability to engage in rational thought and critical analysis. Their philosophical training equips them to understand complex issues and make informed decisions.

5) Altruistic Intent:

The philosopher-king's primary motivation is the well-being of the state and its citizens. They are driven by a sense of duty and a genuine desire to promote the common good.

D) Role of the Philosopher-King:

In Plato's ideal state, the philosopher-king assumes the highest position of authority and governance. Their role involves making decisions that promote justice, harmony, and the overall well-being of the state. Key aspects of their role include:

1) Guardians of Truth:

The philosopher-kings are guardians of truth and knowledge. Their understanding of the Forms guides their decision-making, allowing them to discern the most just and virtuous courses of action.

2) Rule by Wisdom:

Plato believed that a just society could only be achieved if rulers were guided by wisdom rather than personal ambition. The philosopher-kings' decisions are based on a deeper understanding of reality and the principles of justice.

3) Education of Citizens:

The philosopher-kings are responsible for the education and moral development of the citizens. They shape the educational system and oversee the curriculum to ensure that future generations are equipped with the virtues necessary for a just society.

4) Harmony and Order:

The philosopher-kings strive to maintain harmony and order within the state. Their decisions are aimed at preventing conflicts and promoting cooperation among the different classes.

E) Criticisms and Interpretations:

Plato's concept of the philosopher-king has garnered both praise and criticism throughout history:

1) Criticisms of Elitism:

One common criticism is that Plato's philosopher-kings create an elitist ruling class, concentrating power in the hands of a select few. This could lead to a lack of representation and a potential for abuse of power.

2) Practicality and Human Nature:

Critics argue that finding individuals with the necessary qualities for philosopher-kings is highly challenging. Human nature, they contend, is too complex to ensure that rulers will always act in the best interests of the state.

3) Role of Practical Knowledge:

Critics question whether philosophical wisdom alone is sufficient for effective governance. Practical knowledge, leadership skills, and an understanding of economic and social dynamics are also crucial for effective rulership.

4) Interpretation of the Forms:

There are debates about the philosopher-kings' ability to access the world of Forms. The exact nature of their knowledge and how it guides their decisions is subject to interpretation and speculation.

5) Plato's Intent:

Scholars interpret whether Plato intended the philosopher-kings to be an achievable reality or a metaphorical representation of an ideal ruler. Some see them as a utopian aspiration rather than a practical political solution.

★★★

Review Questions

Q. 1. Write Long Answers:

1) Explain the Life and Works of Plato.
2) Discuss about the Plato's Ideal State.
3) Explain the Plato's Justice Theory.
4) Discuss the Plato's Views on System of Education.
5) Explain the Plato's Thoughts on Philosopher King.

Q. 2. Write Short Notes on:

1) Plato's Ideal State.
2) Life of Plato.
3) Work of Plato.
4) Plato's Philosopher King.
5) Plato's Justice.
6) Features of Plato's Education System.

★★★

Thomas Hobbes

2 UNIT

- 2.1 Life and Works of Hobbes
- 2.2 Human Nature
- 2.3 State of Nature
- 2.4 Views on Natural Rights
- 2.5 Theory of Social Contract

Introduction:

Thomas Hobbes (1588–1679) was a philosopher and royalist, educated at Oxford. He spent periods living near Paris, and also travelled round Europe, picking up a wide education in the artistic, scientific and philosophical thinking of the day. He worked as a tutor to the noble and wealthy, but not until his 40s did he start working in earnest on his own philosophical theories. Hobbes wrote many books and contributed too many academic fields, but his 1651 book *Leviathan or the matter, forme and power of a commonwealth ecclesiasticall and civil* is the one he is best remembered for. In addition to political philosophy, Hobbes contributed to a diverse array of other fields, including history, jurisprudence, geometry, theology, and ethics, as well as philosophy in general. He is considered to be one of the founders of modern political philosophy.

2.1 Life and Works of Hobbes:

Thomas Hobbes (1588–1679) was a renowned English philosopher, best known for his influential works on political philosophy and social contract theory. His ideas have significantly contributed to the development of modern political thought and continue to shape discussions on the nature of government, society, and individual rights.

2.1.1 Life of Hobbes:

The 17th Century English philosopher Thomas Hobbes is now widely regarded as one of a handful of truly great political philosophers, whose masterwork Leviathan rivals in significance the political writings of Plato, Aristotle, Locke, Rousseau, Kant, and Rawls.

Hobbes is famous for his early and elaborate development of what has come to be known as "social contract theory", the method of justifying political principles or arrangements by appeal to the agreement that would be made among suitably situated rational, free, and equal persons.

1) **Birth and Family Background:**
   Thomas Hobbes was born prematurely on April 5, 1588, in Westport, Wiltshire, England. He was the son of Thomas Hobbes Sr. and Thomazine, born during a time of political and social tension due to the Spanish Armada's approach.

2) **Turbulent Times:**
   Hobbes grew up during a period of significant turmoil in England, characterized by the English Reformation and conflicts between the Anglican Church and Puritan factions. These tensions would influence his later views on religion and governance.

3) **Education:**
   Displaying intellectual promise, Hobbes attended Malmesbury Grammar School, receiving a solid foundation in Latin and classics that would shape his scholarly pursuits.

4) **University Studies:**
   At the age of 15, in 1603, Hobbes began attending Magdalen Hall at Oxford. He was exposed to Aristotelian philosophy and scholasticism, which dominated intellectual discourse at the time.

5) **Encounters with Notable Figures:**
   During his time at Oxford, Hobbes connected with influential thinkers, including Sir William Cavendish. This connection would become important, as Cavendish would later become a patron and friend to Hobbes.

6) **Tutoring and Travel:**
   Becoming a tutor to the Cavendish family, Hobbes embarked on extensive travels across Europe. These journeys exposed him to diverse intellectual circles, various philosophical perspectives, and the effects of political turmoil.

7) **Intellectual Development:**
   The exposure to European thought and his own experiences during travel contributed to Hobbes' evolving ideas on governance, human nature, and society. These experiences shaped his unique perspective.

8) **Conflict and Controversy:**
   Hobbes' willingness to question religious interpretations and his focus on empirical observation sometimes brought him into conflict with religious and political authorities, leading to concerns about his ideas.

9) **Return to England:**
   In the early 1630s, Hobbes returned to England and settled in London. Engaging with intellectual circles, he continued to refine his philosophical ideas through discussions and debates.

10) Publication of Notable Works:

In 1651, Hobbes published "Leviathan," a seminal work that outlined his comprehensive views on political philosophy, social contract theory, and the role of government in a way that would influence future generations.

11) Legacy and Influence:

The experiences of Hobbes' early life, including his exposure to diverse influences, encounters with prominent figures, and the controversies his ideas sparked, formed the bedrock of his later works and his lasting impact on political philosophy and the understanding of human nature.

2.1.2 Works of Hobbes:

Hobbes wrote several versions of his political philosophy, including The Elements of Law, Natural and Politic (also under the titles Human Nature and De Corpore Politico) published in 1650, De Cive (1642) published in English as Philosophical Rudiments Concerning Government and Society in 1651, the English Leviathan published in 1651, and its Latin revision in 1668. Others of his works are also important in understanding his political philosophy, especially his history of the English Civil War, Behemoth (published 1679), De Corpore (1655), De Homine (1658), Dialogue between a Philosopher and a Student of the Common Laws of England (1681), and The Questions Concerning Liberty, Necessity, and Chance (1656).

1) "The Elements of Law, Natural and Politic" (1640):

One of Hobbes' earliest significant works, this treatise explored his ideas on human nature, society, and government. It laid the groundwork for his later works by discussing the role of reason, the social contract, and the need for a sovereign authority to maintain order.

2) "De Cive" (1642):

This Latin work, translated as "On the Citizen," expanded upon Hobbes' ideas presented in "Elements of Law." It delved into topics like the nature of rights, the social contract, and the structure of government, setting the stage for his more comprehensive works.

3) "Leviathan" (1651):

Hobbes' magnum opus, "Leviathan," stands as a cornerstone of modern political philosophy. It offers a comprehensive exploration of his ideas on the social contract, the state of nature, human motivation, and the necessity of a strong central authority to prevent the chaos of the state of nature. The metaphor of the "Leviathan," a powerful sovereign that represents the collective will of the people, remains central to his philosophy.

4) "De Corpore" (1655) and "De Homine" (1658):

These work, collectively known as the "Body-Politic" trilogy, focus on metaphysics, epistemology, and human nature. "De Corpore" discusses the nature of substance and materialism, while "De Homine" delves into human psychology, perception, and cognition.

5) **"De Cive" (English Version, 1651):**
Hobbes translated and adapted his Latin work "De Cive" into English, making his political and philosophical ideas more accessible to a wider audience. This version contributed to the spread of his influential theories.

6) **"Behemoth" (1681, Posthumously Published):**
Written during the 1660s but published after his death, "Behemoth" provides a historical account of the English Civil War and its aftermath. It reflects Hobbes' political insights into the causes and consequences of the conflict and emphasizes the importance of social order.

7) **"Human Nature" (Written 1650, Published 2016):**
A collection of Hobbes' shorter works, including essays on human nature, ethics, and religion. It offers insights into his thoughts on individual psychology and morality, as well as his critiques of religious dogma.

8) **"Optics" (Written 1640s, Published Posthumously):**
Hobbes applied his keen observations and empirical approach to optics in this work. While not primarily focused on philosophy, it underscores his interdisciplinary interests and methodological rigor.

9) **Correspondence and Dialogue:**
Throughout his life, Hobbes engaged in extensive correspondence and dialogues with other intellectuals of his time, including Descartes and Mersenne. These interactions helped shape his ideas and reflect the ongoing philosophical discourse of the era.

10) **Influence and Reception:**
Hobbes' works sparked significant debates and reactions, both positive and negative. They influenced subsequent philosophers like John Locke and Jean-Jacques Rousseau, who built upon and sometimes challenged his ideas. Hobbes' writings also contributed to the development of liberal and contractualist political theories.

11) **Legacy:**
Hobbes' works left an indelible mark on political philosophy, shaping discussions on the nature of government, the social contract, and individual rights. His emphasis on the necessity of a strong sovereign authority to maintain social order continues to be relevant in modern political thought.

2.2 Human Nature:

Hobbes' conception of human nature is rooted in a pessimistic view that reflects the tumultuous times he lived in, marked by political upheaval and the English Civil War. He famously wrote that in the "state of nature," a hypothetical scenario in which there is no organized society or government, life would be "solitary, poor, nasty, brutish, and short." This grim depiction reflects his belief that in the absence of a central authority, individuals would naturally pursue their self-interests, leading to conflict, insecurity, and violence.

2.2.1 Hobbes Idea of Human Nature:

Thomas Hobbes' views on human nature are characterized by a pessimistic assessment of individuals driven by self-interest and the pursuit of power

1) **State of Nature and Human Behavior:**
   Hobbes' depiction of the state of nature involves a scenario without organized society or government. In this state, individuals exist in a perpetual struggle for self-preservation, where life is characterized by chaos, insecurity, and violence. The absence of a higher authority leaves people to their own devices, resulting in a world that is "solitary, poor, nasty, brutish, and short."

2) **Human Psychology and Motivations:**
   Hobbes believed that at the core of human nature lies self-interest and the pursuit of personal well-being. Individuals are driven to maximize their own pleasure and minimize their pain. This psychological inclination shapes their decisions and actions, as they are naturally inclined to prioritize their own survival and comfort.

3) **Desire for Self-Preservation and Power:**
   Human nature, according to Hobbes, is characterized by two fundamental desires: the desire for self-preservation and the desire for power. The desire for self-preservation drives individuals to ensure their own safety and security, while the desire for power motivates them to seek dominance over others as a means of enhancing their own status and influence.

4) **Competition and Conflict:**
   In the state of nature, Hobbes believed that humans, driven by their self-interested desires, would inevitably compete for limited resources such as food, shelter, and companionship. This competition would lead to conflict, as individuals strive to secure their own interests at the expense of others. The absence of an overarching authority to regulate these conflicts intensifies the struggle.

5) **Natural Equality:**
   Hobbes posited that in the absence of societal hierarchies, humans are naturally equal in terms of physical and mental capacities. This equality contributes to the absence of a natural authority to mediate disputes or establish social order. Without a superior power, individuals are left to navigate their interactions based on their own interpretations of their interests.

6) **Insecurity and Lack of Trust:**
   A key consequence of the state of nature is the pervasive insecurity and lack of trust among individuals. Without a governing body to enforce agreements and

ensure compliance, individuals are skeptical of each other's intentions. This skepticism further fuels the cycle of competition and conflict, as people are wary of being taken advantage of by others.

7) **Social Contract and Consent:**

To escape the turmoil of the state of nature, Hobbes introduced the concept of the social contract. He proposed that individuals would rationally recognize the benefits of cooperation and voluntarily agree to establish a governing authority to maintain order and security. This social contract is based on the consent of individuals who seek to mitigate the inherent risks of the state of nature.

8) **Formation of the Leviathan:**

The social contract leads to the establishment of the Leviathan, a metaphorical representation of the sovereign authority. This centralized power acts as a collective representation of the people's will, holding the responsibility to enforce laws, mediate disputes, and ensure the well-being and security of the society. The Leviathan's authority is all-encompassing, as any division would undermine its ability to maintain order.

9) **Necessity of Strong Central Authority:**

Hobbes asserted that a strong central authority, embodied by the Leviathan, is essential to counteract the inherent tendencies of human nature. The authority's power is crucial to preventing the self-interested pursuits of individuals from spiraling into chaos and perpetual conflict. Without such an authority, Hobbes argued, society would be trapped in an unending cycle of violence and instability.

10) **Absence of Natural Rights:**

In contrast to later thinkers like John Locke, Hobbes did not attribute individuals with inherent or natural rights. Instead, he believed that rights are products of the social contract and are granted by the sovereign authority. Rights are not innate but emerge from the agreement to submit to a higher power for the sake of security and order.

11) **Absolute Sovereignty:**

Central to Hobbes' political philosophy is the concept of absolute sovereignty. The sovereign authority, whether an individual or a collective body, possesses unquestionable power and control over the society. This absolute authority is necessary to prevent internal strife and ensure the stability of the social contract.

12) **Limiting Civil Liberties:**

Hobbes recognized the need for the Leviathan to limit certain civil liberties to maintain order. While individuals relinquish some freedoms under the social contract, the government's authority to limit freedom of speech, assembly, and other rights becomes crucial in preventing dissent and potential disruptions to social harmony.

2.2.2 Critiques on Hobbes of Human Nature:

Critiques of Thomas Hobbes' views on human nature have arisen from various philosophical, ethical, and practical perspectives. While Hobbes' ideas have had a significant impact on political thought, they have also faced challenges and criticisms that highlight potential shortcomings and limitations in his analysis. Some of the main critiques include:

1) **Overly Pessimistic View of Human Nature:**
Critics argue that Hobbes' portrayal of human nature as inherently selfish and prone to violence is overly pessimistic. Many points out those humans are also capable of cooperation, empathy, and altruism. The view that individuals are solely driven by self-interest ignores the complexity of human behavior and the positive aspects of human relationships.

2) **Underestimation of Social Bonds:**
Critics contend that Hobbes underestimated the role of social bonds, relationships, and community in shaping human behavior. He largely overlooked the potential for individuals to form connections and cooperate for mutual benefit beyond mere self-preservation. The importance of family, friendship, and social ties in influencing behavior is often neglected in his perspective.

3) **Limited Historical and Cultural Context:**
Hobbes' views were shaped by the historical context of his time, including the English Civil War and its aftermath. Critics argue that his analysis might not be universally applicable across different historical periods and cultural contexts. Human behavior can be influenced by a variety of factors, including cultural norms, religious beliefs, and economic systems.

4) **Neglect of Moral Considerations:**
Hobbes' focus on self-interest and power dynamics led him to overlook moral considerations and ethical values that play a role in human interactions. Critics argue that individuals often act based on moral principles and a sense of justice, even in situations where personal interests might not be directly at stake.

5) **Authoritarian Implications:**
Hobbes' emphasis on the necessity of a strong central authority with absolute power has raised concerns about the potential for authoritarianism and the suppression of individual rights. Critics worry that his framework could provide a justification for unchecked government control and limit individual freedoms in the name of maintaining order.

6) **Failure to Address Diversity:**
Hobbes' analysis tends to generalize human behavior without acknowledging the diversity of human experiences, perspectives, and motivations. Critics argue that different individuals and groups might exhibit varying degrees of self-interest,

aggression, or cooperation, and these nuances are not adequately addressed in his framework.

7) **Alternative Views of Human Nature:**
Philosophers like Jean-Jacques Rousseau challenged Hobbes' views by proposing that humans are naturally good but corrupted by society. Rousseau's "noble savage" concept suggests that it is societal institutions rather than innate human nature that lead to conflict and inequality.

8) **Inadequate Explanation for Cooperation:**
Critics point out that Hobbes did not adequately explain why individuals would willingly enter into a social contract to establish a governing authority. The motivation for surrendering certain freedoms and rights in exchange for security might not be solely driven by self-interest, and alternative explanations are needed.

9) **Lack of Empirical Evidence:**
Hobbes' views were largely speculative and theoretical, lacking empirical evidence to support his claims about human behavior in the state of nature. Critics argue that his ideas would benefit from more empirical validation or comparison with real-world observations.

10) **Shifts in Modern Societies:**
Some critics contend that the dynamics of human behavior and societal organization have evolved since Hobbes' time. Advances in communication, governance structures, and global interconnectedness have led to new forms of cooperation and conflict resolution that challenge his original assumptions.

2.3 State of Nature:

Thomas Hobbes' views on the state of nature provide a foundational framework for understanding his political philosophy. He portrays the state of nature as a chaotic and conflict-ridden condition characterized by the absence of a central authority. Individuals are driven by self-interest and compete for resources, leading to insecurity and violence. The state of nature serves as the backdrop against which Hobbes develops his social contract theory and the necessity for a powerful sovereign authority to establish order and security.

2.3.1 Hobbes Idea of State of Nature:

Hobbes views about state of nature discuss with following pints:

1) **Definition of the State of Nature:**
Hobbes' concept of the state of nature refers to a hypothetical scenario where there is no established government, laws, or social order. It is a pre-political and pre-social condition in which individuals exist independently, free from the constraints and structures of organized society.

2) **Absence of Central Authority:**

In the state of nature, there is a fundamental absence of a central governing authority to enforce laws, mediate disputes, and ensure order. This lack of a higher power leaves individuals to their own devices, leading to a decentralized and potentially chaotic environment.

3) **Human Nature in the State of Nature:**

According to Hobbes, human nature in the state of nature is driven by the pursuit of self-preservation and personal interests. Individuals act in ways that they perceive will maximize their well-being and security, often without regard for the interests of others.

4) **Natural Equality:**

Hobbes asserts that in the state of nature, all individuals are relatively equal in terms of physical and mental capabilities. This natural equality contributes to the absence of any innate authority that could effectively mediate conflicts or establish social hierarchy.

5) **Competition for Resources:**

Due to the scarcity of resources necessary for survival and well-being, individuals in the state of nature engage in competition for those resources. This competition results from the pursuit of self-interest and can escalate into conflicts and violence.

6) **Insecurity and Fear:**

In the state of nature, the absence of a governing authority creates an environment of insecurity and fear. Individuals lack a reliable means of enforcing agreements, ensuring compliance, or protecting themselves from potential harm caused by others.

7) **"War of All Against All":**

Hobbes famously described the state of nature as a "war of all against all." He argued that in the absence of a central authority to maintain order, individuals would constantly be in conflict with each other, leading to a continuous state of hostility and violence.

8) **Lack of Trust and Cooperation:**

The absence of a central authority also results in a lack of trust and cooperation among individuals. Without mechanisms to enforce agreements and punish breaches, individuals have no incentive to cooperate, and mutual distrust becomes the norm.

9) **Moral and Ethical Ambiguity:**

Hobbes believed that morality and ethics are not inherent in the state of nature. Individuals are guided by self-interest rather than moral principles, leading to a lack of universal standards of right and wrong.

10) Rational Pursuit of Self-Interest:

Hobbes argued that in the absence of external constraints, individuals in the state of nature would rationally seek to protect their own interests. Their actions are driven by a calculated assessment of risks and benefits.

2.3.2 Critiques on Hobbes of State of Nature:

Here are the main critiques of Hobbes' state of nature concept:

1) Simplistic and Unrealistic Assumptions:

Critics argue that Hobbes' depiction of the state of nature relies on overly simplistic assumptions about human behavior. His portrayal of individuals as solely driven by self-interest overlooks the complexity of human motivations, emotions, and moral considerations that play a role in interactions.

2) Neglect of Cooperation and Altruism:

One of the primary criticisms is that Hobbes underestimated humans' capacity for cooperation, altruism, and empathy. Research in anthropology and psychology suggests that cooperation is a fundamental aspect of human nature, challenging Hobbes' assertion that individuals would constantly be in conflict without a central authority.

3) Lack of Historical Evidence:

Hobbes' state of nature is a hypothetical construct without empirical evidence to support its claims. Critics argue that his assumptions about pre-social human behavior are speculative and cannot be validated through historical or archaeological data.

4) Historical and Cultural Diversity:

Critics point out that Hobbes' state of nature assumes a universal human nature without accounting for the diversity of historical contexts and cultural practices. Different societies across time and cultures have exhibited varied forms of social organization and cooperation.

5) Questionable Rationality of Actors:

Hobbes' assumption that individuals in the state of nature act solely out of rational self-interest has been challenged. Critics argue that people often make decisions based on emotions, values, and social norms, which can influence behavior in ways that go beyond pure calculation of benefits and risks.

6) Inadequate Explanation of Conflict Resolution:

Critics contend that Hobbes does not sufficiently explain how conflicts would be resolved within the state of nature. While he emphasizes the "war of all against all," he does not address mechanisms for resolving disputes without a governing authority.

7) **Failure to Address Cultural Evolution:**
Hobbes' concept of the state of nature neglects the notion of cultural evolution and societal development over time. Critics argue that human societies have evolved complex norms, institutions, and systems of governance that challenge the state of nature's perpetual conflict.

8) **Ethical Implications:**
Hobbes' state of nature concept has ethical implications that are contentious. Critics question whether the bleak portrayal of human nature and the need for a powerful sovereign justifies potential abuses of power and suppression of individual rights in the name of order.

9) **Rousseau's Alternative Perspective:**
Jean-Jacques Rousseau presented an alternative view of the state of nature in his work. He argued that humans are inherently good and cooperative, but societal institutions corrupt their behavior. Rousseau's perspective challenges Hobbes' negative outlook on human nature.

10) **Lack of Empirical Falsifiability:**
Some critics argue that Hobbes' theory is not easily falsifiable due to its speculative nature. This lack of falsifiability can limit its scientific validity as a theory about human behavior and social organization.

11) **Limited Scope of Rationality:**
Critics contend that Hobbes' focus on rationality as the driving force of human behavior is overly narrow. Human decision-making is influenced by cognitive biases, emotions, and situational factors that extend beyond rational calculation.

12) **Complexity of Human Motivations:**
Hobbes' emphasis on self-interest as the sole motivation overlooks the multidimensional nature of human desires and motivations. Individuals often act based on a combination of self-interest, social connections, moral values, and personal aspirations.

2.4 Views on Natural Rights:

Thomas Hobbes' views on natural rights diverge from those of many other philosophers, such as John Locke, who argued that individuals possess inherent rights that should be protected by government. Hobbes' perspective on natural rights is a central aspect of his overall political philosophy and is closely tied to his analysis of the state of nature, the social contract, and the role of government. Here's an explanation of Hobbes' views on natural rights:

1) **Absence of Natural Rights in the State of Nature:**
Unlike Locke and other thinkers who believed in the existence of natural rights that individuals possess independently of society, Hobbes did not attribute any natural rights to individuals in the state of nature. He argued that in the absence of

organized society and government, there are no rights that are naturally or inherently guaranteed.

2) **Rights Derived from the Social Contract:**

Hobbes' conception of rights is closely tied to his social contract theory. He believed that individuals willingly enter into a social contract to escape the inherent dangers and conflicts of the state of nature. In this contract, individuals agree to surrender some of their freedoms and rights to a central authority in exchange for security and protection.

3) **Artificial Rights Granted by the Sovereign:**

In Hobbes' theory, the rights individuals have are not innate or inherent; rather, they are "artificial" rights granted by the sovereign authority established through the social contract. The sovereign has the power to determine and enforce these rights as it sees fit, based on the need to maintain order and prevent conflict.

4) **Rights as Authoritative Decrees:**

For Hobbes, rights are essentially authoritative decrees of the sovereign. The sovereign sets the rules and laws that govern the behavior of individuals within the society. These rules define what individuals are allowed or prohibited from doing, shaping the scope of their rights and liberties.

5) **Balancing Rights and Obligations:**

Hobbes emphasized the reciprocal nature of rights and obligations within the social contract. Individuals gain protection and security from the sovereign's authority, but they also have an obligation to obey the laws and directives set by the sovereign. This balance ensures social order and stability.

6) **Limits on Rights for Social Harmony:**

Hobbes believed that the sovereign's authority is necessary to limit certain rights and freedoms that might disrupt social harmony and lead to conflict. The sovereign's power to impose restrictions on speech, assembly, and behavior is essential to prevent dissent and maintain order.

7) **Focus on Order over Individual Liberty:**

Hobbes' emphasis on the need for a strong central authority and the suppression of potential conflicts leads him to prioritize social order over individual liberty. He argued that the surrender of certain rights is a necessary sacrifice to escape the state of nature's chaos.

8) **Critiques and Alternatives:**

Hobbes' view of rights has been criticized for its authoritarian implications and for potentially justifying a government's oppressive control. Other philosophers like Locke countered Hobbes by advocating for the existence of natural rights that individuals possess inherently, regardless of government.

2.5 Theory of Social Contract:

Thomas Hobbes' theory of the social contract is a foundational pillar of his political philosophy, outlined in his seminal work "Leviathan" (1651). Hobbes' theory provides a framework for understanding the origins of political authority, the role of government, and the relationship between individuals and the state. In this theory, he addresses the transition from the state of nature, characterized by chaos and conflict, to the establishment of a social contract that gives rise to a sovereign authority.

A) State of Nature and Human Nature:

Hobbes begins his theory by depicting the state of nature, a hypothetical scenario where there is no organized society or government. In this state, individuals pursue their self-interests, driven by the desires for self-preservation and power. Hobbes famously characterizes the state of nature as "solitary, poor, nasty, brutish, and short," highlighting the inherent conflict, insecurity, and violence that would prevail in the absence of a higher authority. The state of nature serves as a starting point for understanding the necessity of a social contract.

B) Motivation for the Social Contract:

Hobbes argues that individuals, recognizing the dangers and hardships of the state of nature, would rationally seek to escape it by voluntarily entering into a social contract. The social contract is an agreement among individuals to establish a governing authority that would maintain order, protect their lives and property, and secure their well-being. This contract is not a historical event but a theoretical construct used to explain the origin of political authority.

C) Nature of Social Contract:

The nature of Thomas Hobbes' social contract theory is a central aspect of his political philosophy. It outlines the theoretical framework through which individual's transition from the state of nature, characterized by chaos and conflict, to a structured society under the authority of a sovereign power. Understanding the nature of Hobbes' social contract involves exploring its key components, the motivations behind it, the obligations it entails, and its implications for the relationship between individuals and the government. Here's an in-depth analysis of the nature of Hobbes' social contract:

1) Contractual Agreement:

Hobbes' social contract theory is built upon the idea of a contractual agreement among individuals. In the state of nature, individuals are driven by their self-interest and the pursuit of self-preservation. Recognizing the dangers and insecurity of this state, individuals rationally choose to enter into a social contract, relinquishing certain freedoms and rights in exchange for the protection and security provided by a sovereign authority.

2) **Rational Self-Interest:**

Central to Hobbes' theory is the notion that individuals are motivated by rational self-interest. They seek to avoid the state of nature's constant conflict and insecurity and willingly surrender some liberties to establish a more stable social order. This rational calculation guides individuals to make the choice to enter into the social contract.

3) **Formation of the Leviathan:**

The social contract leads to the establishment of the "Leviathan," a powerful and centralized sovereign authority. The Leviathan's role is to maintain order, enforce laws, and prevent conflicts among individuals. It serves as a collective representation of the people's will and holds absolute power to ensure the security and well-being of the society.

4) **Consent and Legitimacy:**

Hobbes' social contract relies on the concept of consent. Individuals collectively agree to submit to the authority of the Leviathan for the sake of security and order. This consent forms the foundation of the sovereign's legitimacy to govern. The legitimacy of the sovereign rests on the voluntary agreement of individuals to obey its commands.

5) **Obligation and Compliance:**

Once the social contract is established and the Leviathan is in place, individuals are morally and legally obligated to obey the laws and directives of the sovereign authority. This obligation is based on the consent given in the contract and the recognition of the sovereign's role in maintaining the stability of society. Failure to comply with the sovereign's commands risks undermining the social contract and reverting to the state of nature.

6) **Balancing Freedom and Security:**

The social contract involves a trade-off between individual freedom and security. While individuals surrender some natural rights and liberties to the sovereign authority, they gain protection from the potential violence and insecurity of the state of nature. This balance between freedom and security is essential for maintaining a stable society.

7) **Authoritative Power of the Sovereign:**

The Leviathan, as the embodiment of the social contract, wields authoritative power to make and enforce laws, settle disputes, and regulate the behavior of individuals. This power is necessary to prevent individuals from returning to their self-interested pursuits, which would lead to conflict and chaos.

8) **Limits on Rights:**

Hobbes' social contract theory acknowledges that individuals relinquish certain rights and freedoms in exchange for the benefits of a structured society. The sovereign authority has the power to limit civil liberties, such as freedom of speech and assembly, when necessary to maintain social order and prevent dissent.

9) Inequality and Obedience:

The establishment of the social contract creates an artificial inequality between the sovereign and the subjects. While individuals are equal in the state of nature, they willingly give up certain rights to the sovereign, creating a hierarchy. Obedience to the sovereign is crucial for upholding the contract and preventing the potential chaos of the state of nature.

10) Focus on Stability and Order:

Hobbes' social contract theory is primarily concerned with achieving stability, order, and security in society. The emphasis on a strong central authority and the suppression of potential conflicts reflects his belief that the social contract is a means to overcome the inherent challenges of the state of nature.

D) Critiques on Hobbes Social Contract Theory:

Thomas Hobbes' social contract theory has generated significant critique and debate from various philosophical, ethical, and practical perspectives. While his theory provides a foundation for understanding political authority and governance, it also faces substantial challenges and criticisms that highlight potential shortcomings and limitations. Here are some of the main critiques of Hobbes' social contract theory:

1) Pessimistic View of Human Nature:

One of the primary critiques of Hobbes' theory revolves around his pessimistic view of human nature. Critics argue that his depiction of individuals as driven solely by self-interest and prone to violence oversimplifies human motivations and behavior. This view neglects the capacity for cooperation, empathy, and moral considerations that also shape human interactions.

2) Authoritarian Implications:

Hobbes' emphasis on a powerful sovereign authority with absolute control has raised concerns about the potential for authoritarianism. Critics worry that his theory could justify a government's suppression of individual rights and freedoms in the name of maintaining social order and stability.

3) Lack of Historical Evidence:

Critics contend that Hobbes' social contract theory lacks empirical evidence to support its claims about the historical process through which the social contract emerged. The absence of concrete historical examples weakens the theory's foundation and leaves it largely speculative.

4) Questionable Voluntary Nature of the Contract:

Some critics challenge the notion that individuals in the state of nature would voluntarily surrender their rights and freedoms to a sovereign authority. They argue that without historical evidence or clear incentives, the concept of voluntary agreement may be unrealistic.

5) **Overemphasis on Fear and Self-Interest:**
Critics point out that Hobbes places excessive emphasis on fear and self-interest as the primary motivations for entering the social contract. This focus overlooks other potential factors, such as moral considerations, shared values, and the desire for social connection and cooperation.

6) **Neglect of Moral and Ethical Considerations:**
Hobbes' theory downplays the role of moral and ethical considerations in human behavior and social interactions. Critics argue that individuals are guided not only by self-interest but also by moral principles, a sense of justice, and a desire for fairness.

7) **Alternative Theories of Cooperation:**
Some critics contend that alternative social contract theories, such as those proposed by John Locke and Jean-Jacques Rousseau, provide more nuanced and optimistic perspectives on human nature and cooperation. These theories challenge Hobbes' assumptions about the need for absolute authority to maintain order.

8) **Limits on Individual Liberty:**
Hobbes' theory justifies limitations on individual liberties in the interest of social harmony and order. Critics argue that this justification could potentially lead to the suppression of dissent and the stifling of individual rights, especially when the government's authority becomes unchecked.

9) **Inadequate Explanation for Cooperation:**
Critics question whether fear and self-interest alone would be sufficient motivations for individuals to cooperate and establish a sovereign authority. They argue that other factors, such as shared values, cultural norms, and historical contexts, could also play significant roles in fostering cooperation.

10) **Lack of Consensus on Social Contract Formation:**
The absence of a clear consensus on how the social contract is formed and how individuals universally agree to it weakens the theory's explanatory power. Critics argue that Hobbes' theory relies on hypothetical scenarios that may not accurately reflect the complexities of human interactions.

11) **Conflict with Historical Evidence:**
Some critics contend that Hobbes' theory does not align with historical accounts of the emergence of governments and political authority in various societies. The diversity of historical contexts and forms of governance challenges the universality of his theory.

★★★

Review Questions

Q. 1. Write Long Answers:

1) Explain the Life and Works of Hobbes.
2) Discuss about the Hobbes Idea of Human Nature.
3) Explain the Hobbes Views on State of Nature.
4) Discuss the Hobbes Vies on Natural rights.
5) Explain the Hobbes Social Contract Theory.

Q. 2. Write Short Notes on:

1) Human Nature.
2) State of Nature.
3) Life of Hobbes.
4) Work of Hobbes.
5) Nature of Social Contract.
6) Critiques on Social Contract Theory.

★★★

John Stuart Mill

3 UNIT

Introduction:

John Stuart Mill was a prominent British philosopher and political economist who advocated for individual liberty, utilitarianism, and women's rights during the 19th century. In his seminal work, "On Liberty," Mill argued passionately for the importance of personal freedom and autonomy. He believed that individuals should have the liberty to think, speak, and act as they wish, as long as their actions do not harm others. Mill emphasized that diverse opinions and open discussion are crucial for societal progress, as they allow for the exploration of new ideas and the correction of errors. He championed the concept of free speech and challenged the idea of societal conformity, asserting that society should not suppress unpopular or dissenting viewpoints. By safeguarding individual liberties, Mill believed that societies could flourish and individuals could fully develop their intellectual and moral capacities.

3.1 Life and Works of Mill:

John Stuart Mill was born in London, May 20th, 1806. His father James Mill was a Scottish philosopher and Economist, who moved in important intellectual circles. The young Mill was educated by his father and Jeremy Bentham – the leading exponent of Utilitarian philosophy. His father hoped that John would become a leading intellect to advance the course of Utilitarianism, and the precious John exceeded his father's hopes and expectations. By the age of eight, he was making strides to becoming fluent in Latin and Greek and becoming very widely read. He also became schooled in the most important economic ideas of the time, such as David Ricardo and Adam Smith.

3.1.1 Life of Mill:

John Stuart Mill was a prominent British philosopher, political economist, and social reformer who lived from 1806 to 1873. His early life was marked by a unique upbringing, intellectual exploration, and a profound influence on his later philosophical and political works. Here is an overview of the early life of John Stuart Mill:

1) **Family Background:**
   John Stuart Mill was born on May 20, 1806, in Pentonville, London, England. He came from a highly intellectual and influential family. His father, James Mill, was a philosopher, economist, and political radical who played a crucial role in shaping John Stuart Mill's education and intellectual development.

2) **Early Education:**
   John Stuart Mill's education began at a very early age. His father believed in an experimental approach to education, which involved exposing young Mill to advanced subjects and ideas. By the age of three, Mill was learning Greek, and by the age of eight, he had studied Latin, logic, and various other subjects.

3) **Utilitarian Influences:**
   James Mill was a follower of the utilitarian philosophy of Jeremy Bentham. This philosophy emphasized the greatest happiness principle, advocating actions that promote the overall well-being and happiness of the greatest number of people. John Stuart Mill was deeply influenced by his father's utilitarian beliefs and later became one of the most important proponents and critics of utilitarianism.

4) **Intellectual Isolation:**
   Mill's early education was intense and focused on intellectual development. However, it also resulted in a somewhat isolated childhood. He lacked opportunities for social interaction with children of his age, which contributed to his intellectual prowess but also led to a sense of isolation.

5) **Autobiography:**
   Mill's "Autobiography," published posthumously in 1873, provides significant insights into his early life. In this work, he discusses his extraordinary education, his relationship with his father, and the challenges he faced in terms of emotional development due to his isolated upbringing.

6) **Mental Health Struggles:**
   Mill experienced periods of depression and mental distress during his early life. The intense education and expectations placed upon him, as well as his lack of social interaction, contributed to his emotional struggles. These experiences later influenced his views on mental health, individuality, and personal liberty.

7) **Later Life Contributions:**
   Mill's early life laid the foundation for his later contributions to philosophy, economics, and political thought. He became a prominent advocate of individual liberty, women's rights, and representative democracy. His works, including

"Utilitarianism," "On Liberty," and "The Subjection of Women," continue to influence debates on ethics, political philosophy, and social justice.

3.1.2 Works of Mill:

Throughout his life, Mill tried to persuade the British public of the necessity of a scientific approach to understanding social, political and economic change while not neglecting the insights of poets and other imaginative writers. Philosophically, he was a radical empiricist who held that all human knowledge, including even mathematics and Logic, is derived by generalization from sensory experience.

1) **System of Logic:**

   His *"System of Logic"* of 1843 was an ambitious attempt to give an account not only of Logic, as the title suggests, but of the methods of science and their applicability to social as well as purely natural phenomena. Mill's conception of Logic comprised not only formal logic (what he called the "logic of consistency"), but also a "logic of proof" (a logic that would show how evidence tended to prove the conclusions we draw from the evidence). This led him to an analysis of causation and ultimately to an account of inductive reasoning that remains the starting point of most modern discussions on Logic. The *"System of Logic"* also attacked the Intuitionist philosophy (the belief that explanations rested on intuitively compelling principles rather than on general causal laws) of William Whewell and Sir William Hamilton, which he saw as "bad philosophy".

2) **Principles of Political Economy:**

   His *"Principles of Political Economy"* of 1848 tried to show that economics was not the "dismal science" that Thomas Carlyle (1795 - 1881) and its radical and literary critics had supposed, and it became one of the most widely read of all books on economics in the period, and dominated economics teaching for decades. His early economic philosophy was generally one of free markets with minimal interventions in the economy, and the *"Principles"* is largely a highly proficient re-statement of Smith and Ricardo's theory of classical capitalist economics. He helped develop the ideas of economies of scale, opportunity cost and comparative advantage in trade. But in the *"Principles"*, Mill also made the radical arguments that we should sacrifice economic growth for the sake of the environment, and should limit population as much to give ourselves breathing space as in order to fend off the risk of starvation for the overburdened poor, and advocated his own ideal of an economy of worker-owned cooperatives.

3) **Utilitanism:**

   His *"Utilitarianism"* of 1861 remains the classic defense of the Utilitarian view that we should aim at maximizing the welfare (or happiness) of all sentient creatures. However, he was keen to develop Utilitarianism into a more humanitarian doctrine. One of Mill's major contributions to Utilitarianism was his argument for the qualitative separation of pleasures, his insistence that happiness should be assessed not merely by quantity but by quality and, more specifically, that intellectual and moral pleasures are superior to more physical forms of pleasure. He went so far as to say that he would rather be a dissatisfied human being than a satisfied pig. He also turned away from Bentham's external standard of goodness to something more subjective, arguing that altruism was as important as self-interest in deciding what ought to be done.

4) On Liberty:

However, it was Mill's essay *"On Liberty"* of 1859 that aroused the greatest controversy and the most violent expressions of approval and disapproval. It addressed the nature and limits of the power that can be legitimately exercised by society over the individual, and he laid down his "one very simple principle" governing the use of coercion in society (whether it be by legal penalties or by the operation of public opinion), arguing that we may only coerce others in self-defense: either to defend ourselves, or to defend others from harm (the so-called "harm principle"). Thus, if an action is self-regarding (i.e. it only directly affects the person undertaking the action), then society has no right to intervene, even if it feels the actor is harming himself. Man is therefore free to do anything unless he harms others, he argued, and individuals are rational enough to make decisions about what is good and also to choose any religion they want.

"On Liberty" also contains an impassioned defense of free speech, arguing that free discourse is a necessary condition for intellectual and social progress, and that we can never be sure that a silenced opinion does not contain some element of the truth. It introduces the concepts of "social liberty" (limits on a ruler's power to prevent him from harming society, requiring that people should have the right to a say in a government's decisions), and also the concept of the "tyranny of the majority" (where the majority oppresses the minority by decisions which could be harmful and wrong sometimes, and against which precautions are needed).

5) Examination of Sir William Hamilton's Philosophy:

Mill's *"Examination of Sir William Hamilton's Philosophy"* of 1865 constituted the first developed presentation of the doctrine of Phenomenalism (the epistemological view which regards sensations as the basic constituents of reality, and attempts to construct the external world from sensations and the possibilities of sensation), and it included his quote: "Matter, then, may be defined as the Permanent Possibility of Sensation". Although the origins of Phenomenalismcan be traced back to George Berkeley, it was only after Mill that a commitment to the doctrine became standard among scientific philosophers, until superseded by Physicalism in the 1930s.

6) The Subjection of Women:

"The Subjection of Women" of 1869, apparently published late in life in order to avoid controversies that would lessen the impact of his other work, was thought to

be excessively radical in Mill's time, but is now seen as a classic statement of liberal Feminism. Mill argued that if freedom is good for men, then it is for women too, and that every argument against this view drawn from the supposedly different "nature" of men and women is based on mere superstitious special pleading. If women do have different natures, the only way to discover what they are is by experiment, and that requires that women should have access to everything to which men have access. He felt that the oppression of women was one of the few remaining relics from ancient times, a set of prejudices that severely impeded the progress of humanity.

3.2 Views on Liberty:

Mill gave importance to individual liberty because there are some reasons which are born out from the circumstances in England. In 1832, Reform Act was passed by the Government of England. It expanded the governmental machinery and increased functions of the state. Simultaneously, there was a demand for more liberty by the people. All these circumstances made liberty of the individual the theme in England in the middle of the 19th Century. In that situation, Mill published his essay “On Liberty”, to defend the case of individual liberty. His book was a powerful plea for individual liberty against the government interference. He said Acts made by the government were tyrannical and interfered in individual freedom. J. S. Mill believes that the government comes into existence for social well-being. Political institutions find their basis in human will and interest. Liberty as a concept Liberty is extremely important in democracy. It is an essential condition for all-round development of human personality.

A) Meaning of Liberty:

Liberty means freedom of an individual. We need liberty to protect ourselves from undue interference of the state. Hence area of action of the state should be limited. Any extension in the activities of the state means erosion of individual liberty. Individualist like Mill believed that the state comes into existence to protect life, liberty and property of the individual. In welfare states; states take up the responsibility of development of an individual and society. Hence, it is essential to have reasonable restrictions on individual. With reasonable restrictions of the state on liberty, everyone can enjoy liberty better. It creates an environment where development takes place. Mill was a great exponent of Liberty. He defended the case of individual liberty in his book “On Liberty”.

B) Importance of Liberty:

Importance of Liberty is as follows:

1) Mill believed that the progress of society depended largely on the originality and energy of the individual. The society would be enriched by the variety of characters in it. Hence, he emphasises that the individual must be allowed maximum liberty to determine his own affairs.

2) Need for the enrichment of individuals personality. If state does not provide them an opportunity to develop and expand their mental faculties, it is neither good for the individuals not for the government. He regarded liberty as the most important principle to protect and promote individuality.

3) Ultimately value of the state depends upon the quality of individuals.

C) Relationship between Liberty and State:

Mill lays down as a general principle that government interference in the activity of individuals should be reduced to minimum. On the basis of utility, he advocated a complete system of individualism. Mill explained the relationship between the state and the liberty of the people as follows: J. S. Mill believed that an individual has two aspects of his life:

1) Individual Aspect:

The individual aspect which concerned him alone.

2) Social Aspect:

In social aspect, every individual is the integral part of society. Accordingly the actions of individual may be divided into two categories, i.e.

a) Self-Regarding Actions:

Individual are sovereign over his own body and mind.

b) Other Regarding Actions:

The actions of the individual, which affect society, can be regulated by the state. It is a social aspect of individual's personality. Here, the society has the right of interference in individual's actions. But this interference must be reduced to the minimum. Any increase in state interference and action is prejudicial to the liberty of the individual and to the development of his personality. According to Mill, state action can mean collective tyranny.

c) Mill was Against Excessive State Interference:

He said state has the right of regulating the actions of individuals which affect the society. The state can compel the individual to perform his duties and obligations as a member of the society. But in actions of the individual which concern him alone, the state should not interfere. The individual should be allowed to carry his opinion into practice at his own cost. The state should not interfere in the affairs of the associations or corporations which affect their members only. The function of the state is to enhance liberty.

D) Mill's Classification of Liberty:

Mill pleads for certain freedoms for the individual without which he cannot develop his personality property. These freedoms are as follows:

1) Negative Liberty:

Negative liberty, as understood by Mill, refers to the absence of external interference or coercion in an individual's actions. It involves the freedom from external constraints that might prevent an individual from pursuing their own goals, desires, and interests. Mill argues that negative liberty is a fundamental and essential component of individual freedom. He advocates for a broad scope of negative liberty, asserting that individuals should be allowed to act as they wish as long as their actions do not harm others.

In the context of negative liberty, Mill emphasizes the harm principle. He argues that the only legitimate reason for society or government to intervene in an individual's actions is to prevent harm to others. This principle places limitations on the extent to which negative liberty can be restricted and suggests that individual autonomy should be prioritized over collective conformity.

2) Positive Liberty:

Positive liberty, on the other hand, pertains to an individual's capacity to pursue their own true interests and develop their potential. It involves the ability to overcome internal obstacles, such as ignorance or lack of education that might hinder an individual's self-realization and self-improvement. While positive liberty may also involve some degree of external support or assistance, Mill is cautious about the potential dangers of paternalism, where authorities or institutions claim to know what is best for individuals and curtail their autonomy in the name of their well-being.

Mill is generally more skeptical of positive liberty compared to negative liberty. He is concerned that well-intentioned interventions aimed at promoting positive liberty might inadvertently lead to the suppression of individual diversity and the imposition of a particular set of values. He argues that individuals should be free to determine their own conception of the good life and pursue their own interests without undue influence or direction from external authorities.

3) Balancing Negative and Positive Liberty:

Mill's views on liberty suggest that negative liberty is the primary concern, as it pertains to the absence of external interference and coercion. However, he recognizes that there can be cases where a certain degree of positive liberty is necessary to ensure that individuals have the conditions and opportunities to exercise their negative liberty effectively. For instance, access to education and economic opportunities can enhance individuals' ability to make informed choices and pursue their goals.

Mill's emphasis on the importance of individuality and self-development aligns with the idea that individuals should have the capacity to exercise both negative and positive liberty. He argues that a society that values individual autonomy and diversity should aim to strike a balance between safeguarding negative liberty and providing conditions that enable positive liberty without infringing on individual autonomy.

E) Criticism on Mill's views on Liberty:

Criticism on Mill's views on Liberty is as follows:

1) Overemphasis on Individualism:

Critics argue that Mill's emphasis on individual autonomy and self-development might lead to a society that neglects communal responsibilities and the welfare of others. They contend that a purely individualistic approach could undermine the sense of social cohesion and shared values that are essential for a well-functioning society.

2) Neglect of Social Goods:

Mill's focus on negative liberty and limited government intervention is seen by some critics as neglecting the importance of social goods and collective interests. They argue that certain public goods, such as healthcare, education, and environmental protection, require government intervention and collective efforts to ensure a just and equitable society.

3) Ambiguity of the Harm Principle:

The harm principle, a cornerstone of Mill's philosophy, has been criticized for its ambiguity. Critics argue that determining what constitutes harm can be subjective and open to interpretation, potentially leading to inconsistent applications of the principle and making it difficult to define clear boundaries for government intervention.

4) Potential for Tyranny of the Majority:

Critics worry that Mill's approach to liberty does not adequately address the potential for the tyranny of the majority. They argue that in a society focused solely on individual rights; minority voices and interests might be suppressed or ignored, leading to a form of majority authoritarianism.

5) Lack of Cultural Sensitivity:

Some critics assert that Mill's framework does not sufficiently account for cultural diversity and variations in values across different societies. They argue that his emphasis on individual autonomy might clash with cultural norms and practices, leading to potential clashes between universal rights and local traditions.

6) Underestimation of Social Influence:

Critics point out that Mill's argument that societal influences should not suppress dissenting opinions underestimates the power of social pressures. They argue that even without government intervention, societal norms and pressures can significantly limit individuals' freedom to express unconventional or unpopular views.

7) Potential for Anarchy:

Critics contend that Mill's stress on minimal government intervention might create a situation of anarchy where essential functions of government, such as maintaining law and order, are compromised. They argue that some level of governmental authority is necessary to ensure the stability and security of society.

8) **Ignoring Socioeconomic Inequalities:**

Critics assert that Mill's approach to liberty fails to adequately address socioeconomic inequalities that can limit individuals' ability to exercise their freedom. They argue that systemic inequalities can effectively constrain the choices and opportunities available to certain individuals or groups.

9) **Relativism and Moral Neutrality:**

Mill's philosophy has been criticized for its potential to lead to moral relativism and ethical indifference. Critics argue that by avoiding making judgments about the inherent value of certain actions or lifestyles, Mill's framework can fail to address broader questions of moral responsibility and the promotion of virtuous behavior.

10) **Limited Role for Government in Promoting Well-Being:**

Some critics argue that Mill's approach restricts the government's ability to actively promote well-being and ensure a higher quality of life for its citizens. They contend that without government intervention, certain public goods and services might be undersupplied, leading to societal deficiencies.

3.3 Views on Representative Government:

Mill began his views on Representative government by stating that we can only decide which the best form of government is by examining which form of government fulfils most adequately the purposes of government. For Mill, a good government performs two functions: it must use the existing qualities and skills of the citizens to best serve their interests and it must improve the moral, intellectual and active qualities of these citizens. A despotic government may be able to fulfill the first purpose, but will fail in the second. Only a representative government is able to fulfill these two functions. It is a representative government that combines judiciously the two principles of participation and competence which is able to fulfill the two functions of protecting and educating the citizens. Mill in his book “Representative Government” suggested reforms for a good Government. He himself was a member of House of Commons in England. He observed some shortcomings in the nature and working of democracy in England. He was a lover of democracy who clarified basic issues and pointed out ways of building up institutions.

A) **Key Aspects of Representative Government:**

John Stuart Mill had profound views on representative government, which he expressed in his seminal work titled "Considerations on Representative Government." In this work, Mill examined the principles, functions, and potential shortcomings of representative democracy, advocating for a more inclusive and participatory form of government. Here are some key aspects of Mill's views on representative government:

1) **Value of Representative Government:**

Mill considered representative government as a crucial element for the well-being of society. He believed that representative institutions allowed for the protection of individual liberties, the prevention of tyranny, and the promotion of the common good. According to Mill, representative government provided a system that could effectively balance individual rights and social welfare.

2) **Importance of Universal Suffrage:**

Mill advocated for universal suffrage, arguing that the right to vote should be extended to all adults, irrespective of gender or property qualifications. He believed that widening the electorate would foster greater political participation, provide a more accurate reflection of public opinion, and prevent the domination of ruling elites.

3) **Protection of Individual Liberty:**

Mill emphasized the need for representative government to protect individual liberties from potential encroachments by both the state and the majority. He argued that democratic governance should include constitutional safeguards and checks and balances to prevent the oppression of minorities and the violation of individual rights.

4) **Pluralism and Free Expression of Ideas:**

Mill championed the importance of pluralism and the free expression of ideas within representative government. He believed that diverse viewpoints and the open exchange of opinions were vital for societal progress and the development of robust policies. Mill advocated for freedom of speech, press, and association as essential components of a healthy democratic system.

5) **Limitations on Majority Rule:**

Mill cautioned against the tyranny of the majority, emphasizing that the mere will of the majority should not automatically prevail in all matters. He argued that certain fundamental rights and principles should be protected even if they go against popular sentiment. Mill suggested that representative institutions should incorporate safeguards to prevent majority oppression and ensure the protection of individual and minority rights.

6) **Education and Political Participation:**

Mill stressed the importance of education in representative government. He believed that an informed and educated citizenry was necessary for active political participation and effective decision-making. Mill encouraged the provision of quality education for all individuals to promote civic awareness, critical thinking, and responsible citizenship.

7) **Role of Representatives:**

According to Mill, representatives in a democratic system should act as the voice of the people and serve the interests of the entire community, rather than pursuing their personal or factional agendas. He called for representatives who were knowledgeable, virtuous, and capable of representing the diverse interests and values of their constituents.

8) Utilitarian Principles in Governance:

While not explicitly tied to representative government, Mill's utilitarian philosophy had an influence on his views regarding governance. He argued that policies and legislation should be assessed based on their overall utility and their ability to maximize the happiness and well-being of the greatest number of people.

B) Reforms in Representative Government:

Mill suggested following reforms in the Representative Government:

1) Voting Rights:

Mill recommended that voting rights should be given to only those who possess a certain amount of intellectual capacity. Mill was not opposed to universal franchise. But he said an enlightened citizen would ensure proper functioning of the government. He advocated educational qualification for voters.

2) Plural Vote:

Mill recommended a system of plural voting to highly educated citizens such as Profs, lawyers. Plural voting means weight age is to be given to education. The persons with greater intelligence and education should have extra votes the judgment of the wiser and more knowledgeable should have a superior weight. Mill was critical of the electoral system which established uniformity instead of recognising the qualities of the individuals. He stressed on plural voting because he had distrust about the lower classes. He does not have much faith in the ability of the average man's capacity.

3) Advocated the Leadership of the Elite Class:

Mill's democracy had an elitist foundation. He said elites alone are capable of bringing in real social and political progress. For him, mass rule is rule by mediocrity. It never ensures progress of a superior quality because masses are ignorant and incompetent and have a poor judgment. Mill advocated in the leadership of the bourgeoisie class. He argued that whatever inequality results out of special treatment to the bourgeoisie class should be tolerated as these better individuals will surely lead society to betterment.

4) Proportional Representation:

Mill supported the system of proportional representation. He was of the opinion that minorities were insufficiently represented in the British Parliament.

5) Open Ballot:

Mill had suggested the implementation of the open ballot system instead of the secret ballot system. In the open ballot system, common men having less knowledge about the political system will be guided by the wiser persons in the society. The assumption behind suggestion was that common people does not understand their responsibilities and generally waste their votes. The system of secret voting would ultimately make the people vote with selfish and private motives. Therefore, he advocated "open ballot".

6) Emancipation of Women and Women Franchise:

Mill paid attention to the question of women's right in the 19th Century. He had a strong plea to end discrimination on the basis of sex. He was the first to raise the issue of women's emancipation in the British Parliament. He said lack of opportunities prevented them from making their contributions to the society. He graved that equality with men in many fields will enable women to make valuable contributions to the society. In the House of Commons, he made an appeal to extend the right to vote to the women. He was in the forefront in the women franchise movement which was getting organised in the latter half of the 19th Century. Mill says, "Women are naturally equal with men and observable differences in their attributes are due to education and circumstances". He was of the opinion that equal educational opportunities should be provided to women. Secondly, their political participation should be increased. He actively supported the women's franchise movement both within and outside the parliament. People's participation in administration and exercise of sovereign authority Mill said every citizen should have a voice in the exercise of that ultimate sovereignty, but he is occasionally called on to take an actual part of the government by the personal discharge of some public functions.

C) Criticisms on Mill's Representative Government:

While John Stuart Mill's views on representative government have had a significant impact on political theory, they have also attracted criticism and generated debates. Here are some key criticisms of Mill's views on representative government:

1) Limited Scope of Representation:

Critics argue that Mill's focus on representative government does not fully address the need for direct participation and involvement of citizens in decision-making processes. They contend that relying solely on elected representatives may result in a detachment between the government and the governed, potentially leading to a lack of accountability and responsiveness to the needs and desires of the people.

2) Insufficient Protection of Minority Rights:

Mill's emphasis on individual liberties and protection against the tyranny of the majority has faced criticism for potentially neglecting the rights of minority groups. Critics argue that representative government, as advocated by Mill, may not provide adequate safeguards to ensure the protection and inclusion of marginalized or disadvantaged communities.

3) Influence of Elite Interests:

Some critics argue that representative government, as envisioned by Mill, may be susceptible to the influence of special interest groups or powerful elites. They contend that the electoral process and the role of money in politics can skew representation and undermine the true voice and interests of the broader population.

4) **Lack of Socioeconomic Equality:**
Critics assert that Mill's views on representative government fail to address the issue of socioeconomic inequality. They argue that political representation alone does not necessarily address economic disparities and may perpetuate unequal power dynamics within society. Without addressing structural inequalities, representative government may not effectively address the needs of the most vulnerable or disadvantaged members of society.

5) **Inherent Bias in the Electorate:**
Critics point out that the electorate itself may be subject to biases, misinformation, or manipulation, which can hinder the effectiveness of representative government. They argue that factors such as limited access to education, media influence, and cognitive biases can distort the decision-making process, potentially compromising the quality of representation and the outcomes of democratic processes.

6) **Fragmentation and Gridlock:**
Some critics contend that representative government, as outlined by Mill, may lead to political fragmentation and gridlock. The presence of diverse interests and viewpoints within representative institutions can make consensus-building and decision-making more challenging, potentially hindering effective governance and policy implementation.

7) **Overemphasis on Rational Deliberation:**
Mill's emphasis on rational discourse and the exchange of ideas in representative government has been criticized for overlooking the influence of emotions, social dynamics, and other non-rational factors that shape political decision-making. Critics argue that this emphasis may not fully capture the complexities and realities of political processes.

8) **Lack of Global Perspective:**
Critics argue that Mill's views on representative government primarily focused on the nation-state level and may not adequately address global governance challenges. In an increasingly interconnected world, they contend that there is a need to consider transnational issues, global inequalities, and international cooperation in discussions on representative government.

3.4 Views on Utilitarianism:

John Stuart Mill, a prominent philosopher and political economist of the 19th century, made significant contributions to the development and refinement of utilitarianism. Utilitarianism is a moral and ethical theory that asserts that the right course of action is the one that maximizes overall happiness or utility for the greatest number of people. Mill's views on utilitarianism, as outlined in his works such as "Utilitarianism" and "Utilitarianism: Second Edition," delve into the foundations, criticisms, and nuances of this ethical theory. In this response, we will explore Mill's views on utilitarianism in detail, addressing key concepts such as the principle of utility, the distinction between higher and lower pleasures, the role of happiness, and criticisms of the theory.

A) Explanation of Mill's Utilitarianism:

Following are the key aspects of Mill's utilitarianism:

1) Principle of Utility:

Mill's utilitarianism is grounded in the principle of utility, which states that actions are morally right if they promote happiness and wrong if they produce unhappiness or pain. The fundamental goal is to maximize overall happiness or utility for the greatest number of people.

2) Consequentialist Ethics:

Mill's utilitarianism is a consequentialist ethical theory, meaning that the morality of actions is determined by their consequences. The focus is on the outcomes or results of actions rather than their intentions or intrinsic nature.

3) Higher and Lower Pleasures:

Mill introduces the concept of qualitative differences in pleasure. He argues that not all pleasures are equal and that there are higher and lower pleasures. Higher pleasures, such as intellectual pursuits and moral satisfaction, are considered superior to lower pleasures, which are more sensual and immediate in nature.

4) Hedonistic Calculus:

Mill acknowledges the need for a method to assess and compare the quantities and qualities of pleasure and pain that result from different actions. He suggests a hedonistic calculus, a system for evaluating the overall happiness or utility generated by different choices. Factors such as intensity, duration, certainty, propinquity, fecundity, purity, and extent are taken into account in this calculation.

5) Intellectual and Moral Development:

Mill argues that the cultivation of intellectual and moral faculties is essential for attaining higher-quality happiness. He believes that engaging in activities that promote personal growth, critical thinking, and virtuous behavior leads to greater overall well-being and fulfillment.

6) Rule Utilitarianism:

While Mill is often associated with act utilitarianism (the assessment of individual actions based on their consequences), he also suggests the concept of rule utilitarianism. Rule utilitarianism proposes that moral rules and principles should be followed as they tend to lead to greater overall happiness when consistently applied. However, in cases where following a rule would lead to less happiness in a particular situation, act utilitarianism should be employed.

7) Individual Rights and Liberty:

Mill incorporates the concept of individual rights and liberty into his utilitarian framework. He argues that individual freedom should be respected and protected as long as it does not harm others. Mill's emphasis on personal autonomy and freedom of thought, speech, and action is a key component of his utilitarian philosophy.

8) **Criticisms of Utilitarianism:**

Mill acknowledges some common criticisms of utilitarianism. For instance, critics argue that it is a doctrine of swine or a philosophy that promotes base pleasures. In response, Mill distinguishes between higher and lower pleasures, asserting that intellectual and moral pursuits are of greater value than mere sensual gratification.

9) **Utility and Moral Progress:**

Mill believes that utilitarianism provides a framework for moral progress and improvement in society. By focusing on maximizing overall happiness, utilitarian principles can guide individuals and societies toward more just, fair, and compassionate actions.

10) **Limitations of Utilitarianism:**

Mill acknowledges that utilitarianism faces challenges in determining the precise measurement of happiness or utility and the difficulty of making accurate predictions about the consequences of actions. He also recognizes that conflicts between the immediate happiness of individuals and the long-term welfare of society may arise.

B) Criticism's on Mill's Utilitarianism:

John Stuart Mill's utilitarianism has garnered both praise and criticism since its formulation. While many recognize its contributions to ethical theory, there are several notable criticisms that have been raised. Here are some of the main criticisms of Mill's utilitarianism:

1) **Neglect of Individual Rights:**

One of the primary criticisms of utilitarianism, including Mill's version, is that it can potentially neglect the importance of individual rights. Critics argue that the focus on maximizing overall happiness may lead to the sacrifice or violation of the rights of certain individuals or minority groups. Utilitarianism's emphasis on the collective good may overshadow the protection of individual liberties and rights.

2) **Inadequate Measurement of Happiness:**

Utilitarianism relies on the measurement of happiness or utility to assess the consequences of actions. However, critics argue that the quantification of happiness is subjective and challenging to measure accurately. Different individuals may have different interpretations and definitions of happiness, making it difficult to establish a universally applicable standard for assessing the overall utility of an action.

3) **Potential for Tyranny of the Majority:**

Critics contend that utilitarianism, in its pursuit of maximizing overall happiness, may give rise to the "tyranny of the majority." Since the theory prioritizes the happiness of the greater number, it can lead to the marginalization or oppression of minority groups or individuals whose interests or well-being conflict with the majority's preferences.

4) **Failure to Account for Intrinsic Value:**
   Utilitarianism has been criticized for its alleged failure to adequately account for the intrinsic value or inherent worth of certain actions, virtues, or moral principles. Critics argue that the theory tends to reduce all values to their instrumental worth in promoting overall happiness, neglecting the importance of actions that may possess inherent moral significance or dignity.

5) **Lack of Moral Integrity:**
   Some critics assert that utilitarianism, including Mill's version, lacks moral integrity or consistency. Since the theory evaluates actions solely based on their consequences, it is argued that it neglects the moral significance of intentions, motives, or the inherent nature of actions. Critics contend that this narrow focus on outcomes may lead to morally questionable decisions if the consequences are deemed favorable from a utilitarian standpoint.

6) **Challenges in Applying Utilitarian Calculations:**
   Critics highlight the practical challenges of applying utilitarian calculations in real-life scenarios. The hedonistic calculus, which attempts to quantify and compare pleasures and pains, is seen as overly complex and subjective. Critics argue that it is difficult, if not impossible, to accurately predict or measure the long-term consequences of actions, making it challenging to make informed utilitarian judgments in practice.

7) **Insensitivity to Individual Preferences:**
   Utilitarianism has been accused of disregarding individual preferences and autonomy. Critics argue that the theory may require individuals to sacrifice their own desires or preferences for the sake of promoting overall happiness, potentially leading to the suppression of personal freedoms and desires.

8) **Lack of Guidance in Decision-Making:**
   Utilitarianism's focus on maximizing overall happiness may provide insufficient guidance in making difficult moral choices. Critics argue that the theory's emphasis on consequences can leave individuals uncertain about which actions are morally right or wrong, as the outcomes are often unpredictable and subject to interpretation.

3.5 Views on State:

John Stuart Mill had complex and nuanced views on the role of the state, which he expressed in his writings on political philosophy. While his views evolved over time, some key aspects of Mill's perspectives on the state include:

1) **Limited State Interference:**
   Mill advocated for a principle of limited state interference in individual affairs. He believed that individuals should have maximum freedom to pursue their own interests and live according to their own values, as long as they do not harm others.

Mill argued for the importance of personal autonomy and individual liberty, and he criticized paternalistic or authoritarian forms of governance.

2) **Protection of Individual Rights:**
Mill emphasized the role of the state in protecting individual rights and preventing the violation of individual liberties. He argued that the state should establish and enforce laws that safeguard people's rights to life, liberty, and property. Mill viewed the protection of individual rights as a fundamental function of the state, and he was critical of any infringement upon those rights by the government or by societal norms.

3) **Utilitarian Role of the State:**
As a utilitarian, Mill believed that the primary purpose of the state was to promote the greatest happiness or utility for the greatest number of people. He argued that the state should intervene when individual actions or market forces produce harm or negative consequences that outweigh the benefits. Mill believed that the state had a role in regulating and mitigating social and economic inequalities to ensure a more equitable distribution of resources and opportunities.

4) **Importance of Democracy and Representative Government:**
Mill considered democracy and representative government as essential for a just and effective state. He believed that democratic institutions allowed for the expression of diverse opinions and prevented the concentration of power in the hands of a few. Mill advocated for universal suffrage, the right to vote, and the protection of individual freedoms within a democratic framework. He saw representative government as a means to ensure the fair representation of citizens and the accountability of those in power.

5) **Education and Social Progress:**
Mill emphasized the role of education in fostering individual development and societal progress. He believed that the state had a responsibility to provide access to quality education to all citizens, enabling them to fully participate in democratic processes and contribute to the advancement of society. Mill saw education as a means to promote rationality, critical thinking, and the cultivation of informed citizens.

6) **Intervention in Public Welfare:**
While Mill advocated for limited state interference, he recognized the importance of the state's role in promoting public welfare. He believed that the state should take an active role in providing public goods, such as infrastructure, healthcare, and education that benefit society as a whole. Mill saw collective action and state intervention as necessary in areas where individual or market mechanisms were insufficient to address social needs or achieve desirable outcomes.

It is important to note that while Mill supported state intervention in certain areas, he also cautioned against excessive state power and the potential for government abuse. He emphasized the need for checks and balances, transparency, and the protection of individual liberties within the functioning of the state.

Overall, Mill's views on the state reflect a balancing act between individual freedom and collective well-being, with an emphasis on the protection of individual rights, the promotion of democratic governance, and the role of the state in addressing social needs and inequalities. His ideas continue to influence discussions on the proper role and limits of government in contemporary political philosophy.

★★★

Review Questions

Q. 1. Write Long Answers:

1) Explain the Life and Works of John Stuart Mill.
2) Discuss about the Thoughts of Mill on Liberty.
3) Explain the Mill's Views on Representative Government.
4) Discuss the Mill's Views on Utilitarianism.
5) Explain the Mill's Thoughts on State.

Q. 2. Write Short Notes on:

1) Types of Liberty.
2) Meaning of Liberty.
3) Life of Mill.
4) Works of Mill.
5) Representative Government.
6) Utilitarianism.

★★★

Karl Marx

4 UNIT

Introduction:

Karl Marx (1818-1883) was the major theorist of` the socialist tradition. He brought together in a powerful theoretical synthesis the key elements of the existing socialist critiques. Even where socialists do not base themselves on the Marxism of Marx, their views are either a reaction to or influenced by it. Once it gained adherents among leaders of the European socialist parties, as it did towards the end of the 1880s, other socialist currents could neither ignore nor avoid its influence. The Bolshevik Revolution of October 1917 seemed to confirm its power, while putting the prestige and resources of a state behind its dissemination. Marx provided socialism with a cogent historical vision, an economic critique of` capitalism on its own terms and an agency of change: the industrial working class. His contribution might be summed up as the materialist conception of history, but its persuasiveness and power can be better appreciated by the term "scientific socialism." It seemed to explain the ills of capitalism and the necessity for socialism at one and the same time. It eschewed the sentimental and visionary and elevated rigor and realism. Marx rejected socialists' stress on moral persuasion of the owners and saw the class of the future indeed, the only really productive class as the working class or "proletariat." The transition to socialism would be a fundamental break from the existing system. But in socialism itself, there would be various stages, the first socialism proper would see the contribution of each to the collective as being rewarded according to how much work was contributed, the ultimate stage communism where each would be rewarded according to need.

4.1 Life and Works of Marx:

John Stuart Mill was born in London, May 20th, 1806. His father James Mill was a Scottish philosopher and Economist, who moved in important intellectual circles. The young Mill was educated by his father and Jeremy Bentham – the leading exponent of Utilitarian philosophy. His father hoped that John would become a leading intellect to advance the course of Utilitarianism, and the precious John exceeded his father's hopes and expectations. By the age of eight, he was making strides to becoming fluent in Latin and Greek and becoming very widely read. He also became schooled in the most important economic ideas of the time, such as David Ricardo and Adam Smith.

4.1.1 Life of Karl Marx:

The German philosopher, revolutionary economist (one who studies the use of money and other material funds), and leader Karl Marx founded modern "scientific" socialism (a system of society in which no property is held as private). His basic ideas known as Marxism form the foundation of Socialist and Communist (an economic and government system characterized by citizens holding all property and goods in common) movements throughout the world.

1) **Early Life:**

   Karl Heinreich Marx was born in Trier, Rhenish Prussia (present-day Germany), on May 5, 1818, the son of Heinrich Marx, a lawyer, and Henriette Presburg Marx, a Dutchwoman. Both Heinrich and Henriette were descendants of a long line of rabbis (masters or teachers of Jewish religion). Barred from the practice of law because he was Jewish, Heinrich Marx converted to Lutheranism about 1817. Karl was baptized in the same church in 1824 at the age of six. Karl attended a Lutheran elementary school but later became an atheist (one who does not believe in the existence of God) and a materialist (one who believes that physical matter is all that is real), rejecting both the Christian and Jewish religions. It was he who coined the saying "Religion is the opium of the people," a basic principle in modern communism.

   Karl attended the Friedrich Wilhelm Gymnasium in Trier for five years, graduating in 1835 at the age of seventeen. The gymnasium's program was the usual classical one history, mathematics, literature, and languages, particularly Greek and Latin. Karl became very skillful in French and Latin, both of which he learned to read and write fluently. In later years he taught himself other languages, so that as a mature scholar he could also read Spanish, Italian, Dutch, Scandinavian, Russian, and English. As his articles in the New York Daily Tribune show, he came to handle the English language masterfully (he loved Shakespeare [1564–1616], whose works he knew by heart), although he never lost his heavy German accent when speaking.

2) **Young Adult Years:**

   In October 1835 Marx enrolled in Bonn University in Bonn, Germany, where he attended courses primarily in law, as it was his father's desire that he become a lawyer. Marx, however, was more interested in philosophy (the study of knowledge) and literature than in law. He wanted to be a poet and dramatist (one who writes plays). In his student days he wrote a great deal of poetry most of it preserved that in his mature years he rightly recognized as imitative and unremarkable. He spent a year at Bonn, studying little but partying and drinking a lot. He also piled up heavy debts.

Marx's dismayed father took him out of Bonn and had him enter the University of Berlin, then a center of intellectual discussion. In Berlin a circle of brilliant thinkers was challenging existing institutions and ideas, including religion, philosophy, ethics (the study of good and bad involving morals), and politics. Marx joined this group of radical (extreme in opinion) thinkers wholeheartedly. He spent more than four years in Berlin, completing his studies with a doctoral degree in March 1841.

3) Forced to move on:

Marx then turned to writing and journalism to support him. In 1842 he became editor of the liberal (open to new ideas) Cologne newspaper Rheinische Zeitung, but the Berlin government prohibited it from being published the following year. In January 1845 Marx was expelled from France "at the instigation [order] of the Prussian government," as he said. He moved to Brussels, Belgium, where he founded the German Workers' Party and was active in the Communist League. Here he wrote the famous Manifesto of the Communist Party (known as the Communist Manifesto). Expelled (forced out) by the Belgian government, Marx moved back to Cologne, where he became editor of the Neue Rheinische Zeitung in June 1848. Less than a year later, the Prussian government stopped the paper, and Marx himself was exiled (forced to leave). He went to Paris, but in September the French government expelled him again. Marx finally settled in London, England, where he lived as a stateless exile (Britain denied him citizenship and Prussia refused to take him back as a citizen) for the rest of his life.

In London Marx's sole means of support was journalism. He wrote for both German-and English-language publications. From August 1852 to March 1862 he was correspondent for the New York Daily Tribune, contributing a total of about 355 articles. Journalism, however, paid very poorly; Marx was literally saved from starvation by the financial support of friend and fellow writer, Friedrich Engels (1820–1895). In London in 1864 Marx helped to found the International Workingmen's Association (known as the First International), for which he wrote the inaugural (opening) address. Thereafter Marx's political activities were limited mainly to exchanging letters with radicals in Europe and America, offering advice, and helping to shape the socialist and labor movements.

4) Personal Life:

Marx was married to his childhood sweetheart, Jenny von Westphalen, who was known as the "most beautiful girl in Trier," on June 19, 1843. She was totally devoted to him. She died of cancer on December 2, 1881, at the age of sixty-seven. For Marx it was a blow from which he never recovered.

The Marxes had seven children, four of whom died in infancy or childhood. He deeply loved his daughters, who, in turn, adored him. Of the three surviving daughters Jenny, Laura, and Eleanor two married Frenchmen. Both of Marx's sons-in-law became prominent French socialists and members of Parliament. Eleanor was active as a British labor organizer.

Marx spent most of his working time in the British Museum, doing research both for his newspaper articles and his books. In preparation for Das Kapital, he read every available work in economic and financial theory and practice.

Marx's excessive smoking, wine drinking, and love of heavily spiced foods may have been contributing causes to his illnesses. In the final dozen years of his life, he could no longer do any continuous intellectual work. He died in his armchair in London on March 14, 1883, about two months before his sixty-fifth birthday. He lies buried in London's Highgate Cemetery, where his grave is marked by a bust (sculpture of a person's head and shoulders) of him.

4.1.2 Works of Karl Marx:

The long history of brutal, totalitarian "Marxist" regimes around the world has left many people with the impression that Marx was an authoritarian thinker. But readers who dive into his work for the first time are often surprised to discover an Enlightenment humanist and a philosopher of emancipation, one who envisaged well-rounded human beings living rich, varied and fulfilling lives in a post-capitalist society. Marx's writings don't just propose a revolutionary political project; they offer a moral critique of the alienation of individuals living in capitalist societies.

1) **An Introduction to a Contribution to the Critique of Hegel's Philosophy of Right :**

Originally published in 1844 in a radical Parisian newspaper, this fascinating short essay captures many of Marx's early criticisms of modern society and his radical vision of emancipation. It also introduces several of the key themes that would shape his later writings. Marx claims that the bourgeois revolutions of the 18th century may have benefited a wealthy and educated class, but did not challenge private forms of domination in the factory, home and field. Marx theorises the revolutionary subject of the working class, and proposes its historic task: to abolish private property and achieve self-emancipation.

2) **Economic and Philosophic Manuscripts of 1844:**

Not published within his lifetime, and only released in 1932 by officials in the Soviet Union, these notes written by Marx are an important source for his theory of capitalist alienation. They reveal the essential outline of what "Marxism" is, and provide the philosophical basis for humanist readings of Marx. In these manuscripts,

Marx analyses the harmful effects of the organisation of labour in modern industrial societies. Modern workers, he argues, have become estranged from the goods they produced, from their own labour activity, and from their fellow workers. Rather than achieving a sense of satisfaction and self-actualisation in their labour, workers are left exhausted and spiritually depleted. For Marx, the antidote to modern alienation is a humanist conception of communism based on free and cooperative production.

3) **The Communist Manifesto:**

The Communist Manifesto in its original edition. Opening with the famous line, "a spectre is haunting Europe – the spectre of communism", the Communist Manifesto has become one of the most influential political documents ever written. Co-authored with Friedrich Engels, this pamphlet was commissioned by London's Communist League and published on the cusp of the various revolutions that rocked Europe in 1848. The manifesto presents Marx's materialist conception of history and his theory of class struggle. It outlines the growing tensions between the bourgeoisie and the proletariat under capitalist relations of production, and predicts the triumph of the workers.

4) **The German Ideology:**

For anyone seeking to understand Marxism's deeper philosophical and historical underpinnings, this is one of his most important texts. Written in around 1846, again with Engels, The German Ideology provides the full development of the two men's methodology, historical materialism, which seeks to understand the history of humankind based on the development of its modes of production. Marx and Engels argue that individuals' social consciousness depends on the material conditions in which they live. He traces the development of different historical modes of production and argues that the present capitalist one will be replaced by communism. Some interpreters view this text as the point where Marx's thought began to emerge in its mature form.

5) **Capital (Volume 1):**

Published in 1867, Capital is Marx's critical diagnosis of the capitalist mode of production. In it, he details the ultimate source of wealth under capitalism: the exploited labour of workers. Workers are free to sell their labour to any capitalist, but since they must sell their labour in order to survive, they are dominated by the class of capitalists as a whole. And through their labour, workers reproduce and reinforce both the economic conditions of their existence and also the social and ideological structure of their society. In Capital, Marx outlines a number of capitalism's internal contradictions, such as a declining rate of profit and the tendency for the formation of capitalist monopolies. While certain aspects of the text have been questioned, Marx's analysis informs economic debate to this day. For anyone trying to understand why capitalism keeps falling into crisis, it's still hugely relevant.

4.2 Views on State:

Marxist theory of state, besides liberal state, is perhaps the most prominent theory. Marxist theory not only challenges the basic concepts of liberal state but also emphasises that it enslaves majority men of society for the realisation of its aims, it is to be abolished or smashed without which the emancipation of common men will never be possible. However, a problem about academic analysis of Marxist theory of state is that nowhere Marx has methodically analysed the theory.

A) Theory of State:

Although Marx and Engels never put forward a unified presentation of the theory of the state, their conception of the state is a fundamental aspect of their outlook and of what has since come to be called Marxism. In fact, theories of the state constitute critical facets of all totalitarian credos, not just the Marxian. After all, a given ideology may be overwhelmingly totalitarian in underlying logic, but if it lacks a focus on using the state as the means of transforming society that is, of imposing its ideas, its totalitarianism will remain implicit. It is the same with Marxism. While Marxism contains many propositions that imply totalitarianism, it is Marx and Engels' view of the state that renders their theory totalitarian in practice. This is most evident in their argument that the state, in the form of the dictatorship of the proletariat, is the chief weapon in the struggle to establish communism. Unfortunately, the totalitarian nature of the Marxist view of the state is not so easily discerned. A glance at Marxist theory and the practice of Marxist organisations will reveal what appears to be a paradox. On the one hand, Marx and Engels and their followers claim to be vigorous opponents of the state and insist that one of their most fundamental goals is the abolition of that institution. On the other hand, the vast majorities of Marxist organisations have been and continue to be, militant advocates of the drastic extension of the role of the state in society. When they have come to power through revolutions or military conquest, Marxists have created societies that have been almost totally dominated by states. Indeed, these states' power has been among the greatest in history. Even the wing of the Marxist movement that no longer aims at revolution, the social-democratic, promotes the systemic expansion of the role of the state in capitalist society. The key to this apparent paradox is the conception of the dictatorship of the proletariat: a state that is supposed to be the vehicle of abolishing the state.

B) Analysis of Marxian State:

Karl Marx, a 19th century philosopher, economist, and political theorist, had complex and evolving views on the state. His ideas on the state were intricately tied to his broader theory of historical materialism and his critique of capitalism. Marx's perspectives on the state are found primarily in his writings, including "The Communist Manifesto" and "The German Ideology." Here, we'll explore Marx's views on the state, its origins, functions, and its role in the context of his larger theoretical framework.

1) **Historical Materialism and the State:**
Marx's understanding of the state is rooted in his theory of historical materialism, which posits that the structure of society, including the state, is determined by the material conditions of production and the resulting class struggles. He believed that the state emerged as a tool of the ruling class to maintain and defend their economic interests and power.

2) **The State as a "Dictatorship of the Bourgeoisie":**
Marx famously referred to the state as the "executive committee of the bourgeoisie" in "The Communist Manifesto." He saw the state as an instrument that serves the interests of the ruling class, particularly the capitalist bourgeoisie. According to Marx, the state enforces laws and regulations that protect private property, ensure the stability of capitalist relations, and suppress any challenges to the status quo.

3) **Role of the State in Class Struggle:**
Marx saw the state as playing a crucial role in mediating and managing class conflicts. He believed that the state's primary function was to maintain the dominance of the ruling class while managing the tensions and conflicts that arise between different classes. The state's legal and coercive apparatus, including the police and the military, serve to protect the interests of the ruling class and ensure social order.

4) **Transition to Communism:**
Marx envisioned a historical trajectory in which the state would gradually wither away as the contradictions of capitalism intensified and class distinctions dissolved. In a communist society, characterized by common ownership of the means of production and the absence of private property, Marx believed that the need for a repressive state apparatus would diminish. With the elimination of class antagonisms and economic exploitation, the state would become unnecessary.

5) **Critique of the State:**
Marx was critical of the state's role in perpetuating inequality and suppressing the working class. He argued that the state, even in democratic forms, served as a tool of the ruling class to protect their interests and maintain their economic power. Marx viewed political freedoms and rights within capitalist societies as illusory, as they were overshadowed by the fundamental economic inequalities inherent to capitalism.

6) **State in the Transition Period:**
In the transitional phase between capitalism and communism, Marx anticipated the emergence of a "proletarian state" that would serve the interests of the working class. This proletarian state, guided by the working class, would carry out the tasks

of expropriating the means of production, dismantling capitalist institutions, and redistributing resources to achieve a more equitable society. However, Marx believed that this state would still retain some elements of coercion and control.

7) **Critics and Interpretations:**

Interpretations of Marx's views on the state vary, and there have been debates among scholars about the nuances of his perspective. Some argue that Marx's theory of the state evolved over time and that he did not provide a detailed blueprint for the structure of the state in a communist society. Others point to Marx's emphasis on class struggle and historical development as key factors that shape his conception of the state.

4.3 Views on Class:

Karl Marx's views on class are central to his overarching theory of historical materialism and his analysis of society and economics. Marx's conceptualization of class is rooted in the relationship individuals have to the means of production and how this relationship shapes their social position, interests, and interactions within society.

4.3.1 Marx Analysis of Class:

His theories on class have had a profound impact on social and political thought, influencing discussions on inequality, capitalism, and the dynamics of social change. Let's explore Marx's views on class in more detail:

1) **Class Defined by the Means of Production:**

Marx's understanding of class is fundamentally economic. He defines class based on individuals' relationship to the means of production, which include resources such as land, machinery, and capital necessary for producing goods and services. According to Marx, the means of production determine who owns and controls economic resources, influencing the distribution of wealth and power in society.

2) **Two Main Classes:**

Marx's class analysis revolves around the distinction between two primary classes: the bourgeoisie (owners of the means of production) and the proletariat (those who sell their labor to the bourgeoisie). The bourgeoisie control the means of production and accumulate wealth through the exploitation of the proletariat's labor, while the proletariat lacks ownership of the means of production and is dependent on selling their labor power for wages.

3) **Exploitation and Surplus Value:**

Central to Marx's understanding of class is the concept of exploitation. Marx argues that under capitalism, the bourgeoisie extract surplus value from the proletariat's labor. The value of goods produced by the proletariat exceeds the wages they are paid. The surplus value is appropriated by the bourgeoisie as profit, perpetuating economic inequality between the classes.

4) Historical Development of Classes:

Marx's theory of historical materialism posits that classes are not fixed entities but are shaped by historical and economic conditions. He identifies various historical epochs characterized by distinct modes of production, such as feudalism and capitalism. Each epoch brings about changes in class structures, relations, and conflicts.

4.3.2 Class Struggle:

Marx's sociology is in fact, sociology of class struggle. According to Bendex and Lipset, "A social class in Marx's terms is any aggregate of persons who perform the same function in the organization of production." According to Marx, "Class is the manifestation of economic differentiation."

A) Concept of Class Struggle:

The concept of class struggle, though not originally propounded by Karl Marx, is yet one of his great contributions to Sociology. To Marx, "the history of all hitherto existing society is the history of class struggle." (The first line of communist manifesto (1848) reads.) According to Raymond Aron, "the classes are the principal actors in the historical drama of capitalism in particular and of history in general."

Classes refer to the groups of people having their own role to play in the relations of production. Relations of production refer to the fact that in the process of industrial production the labour and capital stands in specific relation to each other. Labour is the capacity which the working class possesses. Capital is the instrument invested out of which profit is derived. Those who possess capital they are the owners of capital. Those who are labourers they are the owners of labour power. Capital gets profit, labour gets wage. Labour and capital are interrelated, they are inseparable. One cannot be thought of without the other.

Classes are hence the groups of people identified and distinguished from each other on the basis of their relations to the economic means of production. Economic means of production refers to the economic infrastructure that few people own as against many. Few people are capitalists and many are labourers. Economic infrastructure refers to all those land, machinery, tools, technology and the skills that assist the process of production.

B) The Class Structure:

The word "class" originated from the Latin term "Classis" a group called to arms, a division of the people. In the rule of legendary Roman king, Servius Tullius (678-534 B.C), the Roman society was divided into five classes or orders according to their wealth. Subsequently the word 'class' was applied to large groups of people into which human society came to be divided.

Marx recognized class as a unique feature of capitalist societies. Marx has used the term Social class throughout his works but explained it only in a fragmented form. The clearest passages on the concept of class structure can be found in the third volume of his famous work Capital (1894). Under the title of "Social classes", Marx distinguished three classes related to the three sources of income.

1) Owners of simple labour power or labourers whose main source of income is labour.

2) Owners of capital or capitalists whose main source of income is profit or surplus value.

3) Landowners whose main source of income is ground rent.

In this way the class structure of modern capitalist society is composed of three major classes' i.e. salaried labourers of workers, capitalists and landowners. At a broader level, society could be divided into two major classes - Haves and Have-nots. Haves are the owners of land/or capital often called as Bourgeoisie and the Have-nots are those who own nothing but their own labour power, often called as Proletariates. According to Marx, "a social class occupies a fixed place in the process of production."

Bendex and Lipset have identified five variables that determine a class in the Marxian sense:

a) Conflicts over the distribution of economic rewards between the classes.

b) Easy communication between the individuals in the same class position so that ideas and action programs are readily disseminated.

c) Growth of class consciousness in the sense that the members of the class have a feeling of solidarity and understanding of their historical role.

d) Profound dissatisfaction in the lower class over its inability to control the economic structure of which it feels itself to be the exploited victim.

e) Establishment of a political organization resulting from the economic structure, the historical situation and maturation of class-consciousness.

C) Criteria for Determination of Class:

A social class has two major criteria:

1) Objective Criteria:

People sharing the same relationship to the means of production comprise a class. For example, all labourers have a similar relationship with the land owners. On the other hand all the landowners as a class have a similar relationship with the land and labourers. In this way, labourers on one hand and land owners on the other hand could be seen as classes. However, for Marx, this relationship is not sufficient to determine the class. Because according to him it is not sufficient for class to be "Class in it' but it should also be "Class for itself". Marx means by "Class in itself' the objective criteria of any social class. He is not satisfied with the objective criteria. Hence, he equally emphasizes upon the other major criteria i.e. "class for itself' or the subjective criteria.

2) Subjective Criteria:

Any collectivity of human grouping with a similar relationship would make a category not a class, if subjective criteria are not included. The members of any one class not only have similar consciousness but they also share a similar consciousness of the fact that they belong to the same class.

This similar consciousness of a class serves as the basis for uniting its members for organising social action. Here this similar consciousness towards acting together for their common interest is what Marx class-"Class for itself." In this way these two criteria together determine a class and class structure in any given society.

D) Classification of Societies in History and Emergence of Classes:

Marx differentiated stages of human history on the basis of their economic regime or modes of production. He distinguished four major modes of production:

a) The Asiatic
b) The Ancient
c) The Feudal
d) The Capitalistic

He predicted that all social development will culminate into a stage called Communism.

1) He simplified this classification of societies or various stages of human history into:
2) Primitive-Communal
3) Slave-owning
4) Feudal
5) Capitalist
6) Communist stage.

E) Criticisms on Marx Theory of Class Struggle:

Here are some of the critiques on Marx's idea of class struggle:

1) Oversimplification of Social Dynamics:

Critics argue that Marx's model of class struggle oversimplifies the complexity of social interactions and conflicts. Society is composed of numerous intersecting identities and interests beyond economic class, such as race, gender, ethnicity, and culture. Focusing solely on class relations may disregard the influence of these other factors on individuals' experiences and struggles.

2) Limited Historical Accuracy:

Critics contend that history has not consistently followed Marx's predictions of class struggle leading to a proletarian revolution. Historical events have shown that various factors beyond pure economic class dynamics contribute to social change, making it difficult to attribute revolutionary outcomes solely to class struggle.

3) Neglect of Cooperation and Collaboration:

Marx's emphasis on conflict and struggle between classes can downplay the potential for cooperation and collaboration within and across classes. Critics argue that human societies also exhibit instances of cooperation, shared interests, and alliances that go beyond the antagonistic relationship between bourgeoisie and proletariat.

4) **Ignoring Gradual Reforms:**
Marx's theory tends to focus on revolutionary change and the overthrow of the capitalist system. Critics argue that this perspective disregards the potential for gradual reforms that can lead to improved working conditions, rights for workers, and wealth redistribution without necessarily dismantling the entire capitalist structure.

5) **Cultural and Ideological Influences:**
Critics contend that Marx's theory places less emphasis on cultural and ideological influences that shape individuals' beliefs and actions. Cultural factors can impact class consciousness and the degree of solidarity within the working class, potentially altering the trajectory of class struggle.

6) **Global Variation in Class Dynamics:**
Marx's theory emerged from a specific historical context in Europe during the Industrial Revolution. Critics argue that its applicability to different global contexts and societies with varying economic and cultural conditions may be limited, as class dynamics can manifest differently in different regions and time periods.

7) **Fluidity of Class Boundaries:**
Critics question the assumption that class divisions are rigid and fixed. In reality, individuals can move between classes due to factors such as education, entrepreneurship, and social mobility. This fluidity challenges the notion of an unchanging, inherently antagonistic relationship between the bourgeoisie and proletariat.

8) **Economic Determinism:**
Critics argue that Marx's theory is overly deterministic, implying that economic factors solely determine social outcomes. This perspective neglects the agency of individuals and the influence of political decisions, cultural shifts, and technological advancements in shaping society.

9) **Lack of Attention to Non-Economic Power Structures:**
Critics assert that Marx's focus on economic class relations neglects the influence of non-economic power structures, such as the state, religion, and culture, in shaping societal dynamics. These factors can significantly impact class struggles and outcomes.

4.4 Historical Materialism:

An exercise to understand historical/social developments by employing the tool of dialectical materialism is known as historical materialism in Marxist terminology. Some Marxist scholars prefer to call it materialistic interpretation of history. It is obvious that material conditions, for instance geographical realities, do influence the course of social development. However, according to historical materialism, the impact of geographical environment is not of a seminal nature because social changes appear at much faster pace than the changes and development of geographical phenomena. Citing from European history Marx pointed out that during the last three thousand years, three different social systems appeared viz., the primitive communal system, the slave system and the feudal system. However, during the same period geographical environment almost remained as it was in the past and whatever changes that took place in geographical realities of Europe were insignificant.

A) Meaning of Historical Materialism:

Marx's general ideas about society are known as his theory of historical materialism. Materialism is the basis of his sociological thought because, for Marx, material conditions or economic factors affect the structure and development of society. His theory is that material conditions essentially comprise technological means of production and human society is formed by the forces and relations of production. It is historical because Marx has traced the evolution of human societies from one stage to another. It is called materialistic because Marx has interpreted the evolution of societies in terms of their material or economic bases. Materialism simply means that it is matter or material reality, which is the basis for any change. The earlier view that of Hegel was that ideas were the cause of change. Marx opposed this view and instead argued that ideas were a result of objective reality, i.e., matter and not vice versa.

In his efforts to understand society in its entirety, he has not confined himself to examining the structure of human societies at a given point of time. He has explained the societies in terms of the future of humankind. For him, it is not enough to describe the world. He has a plan for changing it. Thus, his sociological thinking largely concerns the mechanism of change. To understand social change, he has derived its phases from the philosophical ideas of Hegel, the German philosopher.

To turn back to Marx's theory of historical materialism, you need to look at it as Marx's general theory of society, which deals extensively with the contradictions found in the capitalist societies of his times. According to Friedrich Engels the theory of historical materialism was discovered by Karl Marx, but Marx thought it was Friedrich Engels who had conceived Historical Materialism the materialist formulation of history independently. We shall say that both of them used this theory, to quote Marx, as the 'guiding thread' of all their works.

In Engels' view, the theory of historical materialism takes a special view of history. In this view, Engels seeks the final cause and the spirit behind historical events. Both Karl Marx and Friedrich Engels stress the scientific nature of their views of history. In the German Ideology, Marx and Engels assert that their views of history are based on observation and an exact description of actual conditions.

B) Historical Stages of Growth:

Thus, according to historical materialism five types of relations of production are identified in history viz. primitive communal, slave, feudal, capitalist and socialist.

1) Primitive Communism:

Primitive communism is the first stage. It was characterised by a classes society, were in all factors of production was owned in common and people lived in groups. The ancient communal and State ownership which proceeds especially from the union of several tribes into a city by agreement or by conquest. During this stage, the concept of private property begins to develop, "With the development of private property, we find here for the first time the same conditions which we shall find again, only on a more extensive scale, with modern private property. On the one hand, the concentration of private property, on the other hand, coupled with this, the transformation of the plebeian small peasantry into a proletariat".

2) Slavery:

Gradually, a society having a few masters and many slaves remaining under the control of masters came into existence. With the development of productive forces, feudalism replaced slavery. In this stage, all the work is done by human labour like hunting, preparing shelter, finding skin of animals or bark of a tree to be used as cloths. This made the human labour the most important resource which can earn income. Those who had maximum slaves were the most powerful in the society.

3) Feudalism:

Under feudalism there were two classes namely, feudal lords and serfs. On account of friction between these two classes' namely feudal lords and serfs, this system comes to an end. Serfs agitate and get emancipated from feudal lord ultimately feudalism gives way to capitalism. Merchants and entrepreneurs become leaders in the economic field.

4) Capitalism:

Industrial revolution and other changes which took place at the same time gave a new phase time gave a new phase to the economic system which was taking a definite shape at that time. In this atmosphere, a new class of workers (proletariat) emerged against the class of capitalist. The conflicting interest of these two classes is important features of capitalism. There has always been a clash of interest between these two classes. This class conflict according to Marx is the cause of the collapse of capitalism and the rise of socialism.

5) Socialism and Communism:

Maturity of capitalism will create intense class conflict between proletariat (labour class) and bourgeois (capitalist class). Ultimately, labour will unite together and over the state controlled by capitalist class through a revolution. In a socialistic economy, labour will control the state and will own the companies. Market mechanism will be substituted by planning by the state. Income of the individuals will be decided by their needs and not by market mechanism. Ultimately socialism will lead to communism whereby state itself and there will be no shortage of products. "Capitalism sows the seeds of its own destruction". Thus, class conflict is the mechanism of social change. Under the new social order- socialism, economic condition of the working class is improved according to Marxian theory of development communism emerges as the last stage of socialism. Under communism:

a) Poverty is rooted out.
b) Class conflict is absent.
c) Every individual contributes to national income. According to his abilities and receives according to his abilities and receives according to his needs.
d) Above all the state withers away.

According to the Marxian theory of economic development, any social system based on class conflict cannot be a permanent system. So capitalism is to be considered as a transition state in the evolution of society. The capitalist controls the means of production and the workers depend on the capitalist for work. The main aim of the capitalist for work, the main aim of the capitalist is to maximise their profits. This they do by exploitation of labour pay low wages, long hours of work and employment of women and children are some of the ways by which a capitalist exploit workers. As exploitation increases, conditions become ripe to overthrow of capitalism by the united proletariat. Thus, increasing antagonism between capitalist and workers creates conditions for the destruction of capitalism, the emergence of socialism. Here lies the importance of class conflict in the Marxian development model.

C) Principles of Historical Materialism:

Karl Marx's historical materialism is a foundational concept in his broader philosophical and political framework. It provides a lens through which he analyzes the development of societies, the role of economic forces, and the dynamics of social change. The principles of historical materialism encompass several key ideas that together form a comprehensive theory of historical development. Here are the main principles of Marx's historical materialism:

1) Materialist Basis of Society:

Historical materialism is grounded in the idea that the material conditions of production and distribution of resources shape the structure and development of societies. Marx believed that the fundamental aspect of human life is the production of the means of subsistence, which involves not only technology but also the social relations through which people produce and exchange goods.

2) Dialectical Approach:

Marx's historical materialism is dialectical in nature. It draws on dialectical reasoning, which involves the interaction of opposing forces or contradictions. Marx applied this approach to historical processes, viewing history as a result of the dialectical interplay between opposing forces such as class struggle, economic interests, and social contradictions.

3) **Modes of Production:**

Marx identified different historical epochs, or modes of production, characterized by distinct ways in which societies organize production, distribution, and ownership of resources. These modes of production include primitive communism, slave societies, feudalism, capitalism, and his envisioned future mode of production, communism.

4) **Base and Superstructure:**

Marx's historical materialism introduces the concept of the "base" and the "superstructure." The base refers to the economic foundation of society, including the means of production and the relationships of production. The superstructure encompasses the cultural, political, legal, and ideological aspects of society that arise from the economic base.

5) **Class Struggle:**

Marx's theory of historical materialism places a strong emphasis on class struggle as the driving force behind historical change. He believed that history is characterized by conflicts between different classes with conflicting interests, such as the bourgeoisie (owners of the means of production) and the proletariat (working class).

6) **Change and Revolution:**

According to historical materialism, societies undergo change as a result of the contradictions and conflicts within their modes of production. Marx believed that these contradictions would eventually lead to revolutionary transformations that replace existing modes of production with new ones. For example, he predicted that capitalism would be replaced by communism through a proletarian revolution.

7) **Role of Ideology:**

Marx's theory recognizes the influence of ideology, which he saw as arising from the economic base and serving the interests of the ruling class. Ideology includes beliefs, values, and institutions that legitimize and reinforce the existing social order. Marx believed that in capitalist societies, ideology can obscure class interests and maintain the status quo.

8) **Transition to Communism:**

A central aspect of Marx's historical materialism is the transition from capitalism to communism. He envisioned communism as the final stage of human history, characterized by the abolition of private property, class distinctions, and the establishment of a classless society where resources are collectively owned and distributed according to needs.

D) Critiques on Historical Materialism:

Here are some of the key critiques on Marx's historical materialism:

1) Economic Determinism:

Critics argue that historical materialism can be overly deterministic, suggesting that economic factors alone determine historical development. This perspective neglects the complex interplay of cultural, political, and ideological forces that also shape societies and historical change.

2) Oversimplification of History:

Marx's framework categorizes historical epochs based on their dominant modes of production. Critics contend that this oversimplification fails to capture the intricate historical realities and variations within societies. Different societies may have experienced multiple modes of production simultaneously, leading to complex social dynamics that Marx's model does not fully account for.

3) Neglect of Non-Economic Factors:

Historical materialism places a primary emphasis on economic factors, often overshadowing the influence of non-economic forces such as cultural values, religion, and political institutions. Critics argue that these non-economic factors play a significant role in shaping societies and historical processes.

4) Universality and Eurocentrism:

Critics assert that Marx's historical materialism may be Eurocentric in its focus on European history and the evolution of capitalism. The applicability of his model to non-European societies and their unique historical trajectories is questioned, as they may not neatly fit into the stages of development outlined by Marx.

5) Linear Progression:

Marx's theory implies a linear progression of historical stages, from primitive communism to socialism and communism. Critics argue that this progression ignores the potential for societies to move back and forth between different stages or to experience multiple forms of production simultaneously.

6) Role of Ideas and Culture:

Marx's historical materialism downplays the role of ideas, culture, and ideology in shaping societies. Critics contend that cultural and ideological factors can have a significant impact on historical change, influencing individuals' beliefs, values, and actions.

7) Ignoring Peaceful Change:

Marx's focus on class struggle and revolutionary change ignores the potential for peaceful reform and incremental improvements within existing systems. Critics argue that this perspective overlooks instances where social change occurs through negotiations, compromise, and gradual reforms.

8) **Neglect of Positive Aspects of Capitalism:**
Critics suggest that Marx's historical materialism tends to emphasize the negative aspects of capitalism while neglecting its role in driving technological innovation, economic growth, and improvements in living standards for many people.

9) **Lack of Predictive Power:**
Marx's historical materialism has been criticized for its limited predictive power. Some argue that it failed to anticipate certain historical developments, such as the rise of social welfare programs and the emergence of middle classes in capitalist societies.

10) **Complexity of Class Relations:**
Critics contend that class relations can be more complex than Marx's binary classification of bourgeoisie and proletariat suggests. They argue that there are intermediary classes and overlapping interests that challenge the simplicity of the class struggle model.

4.5 Views on Revolution:

Karl Marx, a 19th-century philosopher, economist, and political theorist, is perhaps best known for his views on revolution. His ideas on revolution are central to his larger framework of historical materialism and his critique of capitalism. Marx's perspectives on revolution are articulated in various works, including "The Communist Manifesto" (co-authored with Friedrich Engels) and his writings on class struggle and historical development. In this essay, we will delve into Marx's views on revolution, examining his theories, arguments, and the implications of his revolutionary vision.

1) **Historical Materialism and the Necessity of Revolution:**
At the heart of Marx's views on revolution is his theory of historical materialism. Marx believed that societies evolve through distinct stages of development driven by the contradictions within their economic systems. Capitalism, in particular, is characterized by inherent contradictions between the bourgeoisie (owners of the means of production) and the proletariat (working class). Marx argued that these contradictions would inevitably lead to class struggle and, ultimately, to revolutionary change. Marx saw revolution as a natural outcome of the intensifying class conflicts within capitalism. He believed that the inherent exploitation of the proletariat by the bourgeoisie would create a revolutionary consciousness among the working class, prompting them to rise against their oppressors and establish a new social order.

2) **Proletarian Revolution and the Abolition of Capitalism:**
Marx's vision of revolution centers on the idea of a proletarian revolution, in which the working class collectively rises against the bourgeoisie and seizes control of the means of production. He argued that the proletariat, having nothing to lose but their chains would unite to overthrow the capitalist system and establish a classless

society. According to Marx, the proletarian revolution would lead to the abolition of private property, the means of production being collectively owned, and the end of class distinctions. This transition would mark the shift from capitalism to socialism, with the working class taking control of society's productive forces and directing them toward the common good.

3) **Role of Class Struggle:**

Marx believed that class struggle was the engine of historical change and the driving force behind revolution. He saw the working class as a revolutionary agent that, through its organized efforts and solidarity, would challenge the dominant capitalist class and eventually overthrow it. Marx's concept of "class consciousness" refers to the awareness among the working class of their shared interests and the recognition of their role in effecting revolutionary change. Marx saw periods of heightened class struggle, often marked by strikes, protests, and conflicts, as precursors to revolutionary moments. He viewed these struggles as transformative, as they serve to unite the working class, expose the contradictions of capitalism, and prepare the ground for revolutionary action.

4) **Transition to Communism:**

For Marx, the proletarian revolution was not an end in itself but a means to achieve the ultimate goal of communism. He envisioned communism as a classless and stateless society in which the means of production are collectively owned and controlled by the workers. In a communist society, resources would be distributed according to the principle of "from each according to his ability, to each according to his needs." Marx believed that communism would represent a higher stage of human development, characterized by the elimination of economic exploitation, the withering away of class distinctions, and the harmonious cooperation of individuals for the betterment of all.

5) **Critiques of Capitalism and Revolutionary Praxis:**

Marx's views on revolution were rooted in his scathing critique of capitalism. He highlighted the alienation of workers from the products of their labor, the commodification of human labor under capitalism, and the concentration of wealth and power in the hands of a few capitalists. Marx argued that capitalism's inherent contradictions would lead to its downfall and pave the way for a more just and equitable society.

6) **Historical Context and Interpretations:**

Critics and scholars have debated the extent to which Marx's predictions about revolution have materialized. Some argue that Marx's analysis accurately captures certain aspects of capitalist dynamics, such as economic inequality and exploitation, while others question the inevitability of a proletarian revolution and the feasibility of a transition to communism. It is important to note that Marx's ideas on revolution were developed in the context of the 19th century, influenced by the socio-economic conditions of the Industrial Revolution and the emergence of modern capitalism. The historical context in which he wrote has led to varying interpretations of his revolutionary theories and their relevance to contemporary society.

★★★

Review Questions

Q. 1. Write Long Answers:

1) Explain the Life and Works of Karl Marx.
2) Discuss about the Marx Thoughts on State.
3) Explain the Marx Views on Class.
4) Discuss the Marx Class Struggle Theory.
5) Explain the Marx Thoughts on Historical Materialism.
6) Explain the Marx Views on Revolution.

Q. 2. Write Short Notes on:

1) Types of State.
2) Concept of Class.
3) Class Struggle.
4) Life of Marx.
5) Works of Marx.
6) Historical Stages of Growth.
7) Revolution.

★★★